May 2014

ALIVE!

Extraordinary Stories of
Ordinary People Who Survived
Deadly Tornadoes, Avalanches,
Shipwrecks, and More

Reader's
digest

The Reader's Digest Association, Inc.
New York, NY / Montreal

A READER'S DIGEST BOOK

Copyright © 2014 The Reader's Digest Association, Inc.

The credits that appear on pages 215 are hereby made part of this copyright page.

Library of Congress Cataloging-in-Publication Data
Alive! : extraordinary stories of ordinary people who survived deadly
tornadoes, avalanches, shipwrecks and more! / editors of Reader's Digest.
    pages cm
   Summary: "Alive! is a heart-stopping collection of survival stories from
the archives of Reader's Digest's 'Drama in Real Life' series"-- Provided by
publisher.
  ISBN 978-1-62145-161-7 (hardback) -- ISBN 978-1-62145-162-4 (epub)
  1. Disasters--Literary collections. 2. Disaster victims--Literary collections.
I. Reader's Digest Association.
  PN6071.D56A45 2014
  808.8'036--dc23
                          2013046437

We are committed to both the quality of our products and the service we
provide to our customers. We value your comments, so please feel free to
contact us.
          The Reader's Digest Association, Inc.
          Adult Trade Publishing
          44 South Broadway
          White Plains, NY 10601

For more Reader's Digest products and information, visit our website:
          www.rd.com (in the United States)
          www.readersdigest.ca (in Canada)

Printed in the United States of America

10 9 8 7 6 5 4 3 2 1

CONTENTS

AT THE MERCY OF A WILD ANIMAL

INTRODUCTION

The will to survive is a primal human instinct and one that, we hope, will kick in exactly when we need it most. Whether we are adrenaline junkies looking for a rush or enjoying a mellow weekend outing, or perhaps just in the wrong place at the wrong time, we hope that when faced with a life-threatening situation we will be able to dig deep into our reserves and survive.

Reader's Digest has chronicled such life and death tales in its iconic and popular feature "Drama in Real Life." These stories have kept readers on the edge of their seats and inspired many with images of resilience and bravery that maintain our faith in the human spirit. You'll be awed as you watch a teenager escort his eighty year old grandmother through a raging wildfire to safety; you'll hold your breath as a mountain climber falls into a crevasse on Mt. McKinley and must drag himself to safety, knowing his partner did not survive the fall; and your heart will pound as a hiker comes face to face with an angry mountain lion on a lonely trail.

We hope you'll enjoy these timeless adventure stories and be reminded that even ordinary people are capable of extraordinary things when their lives are on the line.

FACING
MOTHER NATURE'S
FURY

SUPER STORM

BY CHRISTOPHER W. DAVIS

National Weather Service Storm Prediction Center Norman, Oklahoma Saturday, April 1, 2006 11:59 p.m.: Warm front extending across Missouri into the southeastern U.S. . . . Moist, unstable air, mid-Mississippi region. Possible tornadoes.

Sunday, April 2, 2006, 5:30 p.m. Dyer County, Tennessee.
The picture windows in Rick and Laura Gregory's home looked west over cotton fields toward the Mississippi River and the boot heel of Missouri beyond. As the sun went down, it played tricks with the sky, painting it yellow and orange. The news crawl at the bottom of the TV screen in the Gregorys' family room said "Tornado watch."

Laura was in the kitchen preparing an early dinner. Her husband, Rick, a patrol sergeant for Dyer County, had just come off duty. If a storm struck, he'd have to go back out again. She wanted to get some food in him first.

Then the newscasters came on to report that a tornado had

hit Marmaduke, Arkansas, 60 miles to the west. When they started talking about Caruthersville, directly across the Mississippi, Rick was sure they were in for it. He quickly finished his supper. Without a storm cellar, people said, the bathroom was the safest place. He turned to Laura and told her to get theirs ready. If you hunker down in the tub with a cell phone, a candle and a battery-powered radio, you'll be okay. What Rick was about to see over the next 48 hours would change that belief forever.

The previous weekend, Vanice and Larry Parker had moved into their new ranch house with cypress wood siding on Meacham Road. They'd taken their time building, adding custom touches to the house and a large cabinetry workshop in the side yard. Having lived down the road for ten years, they already knew their new neighbors by sight—Janie King, the Hickmans, and the McAndrews.

Vanice and Larry had spent most of Sunday rearranging furniture, trying different configurations for the dining and living room areas. They unpacked boxes and planted a few trees. The day was unusually warm for April, so Vanice opened the windows in the living room. There was a nice breeze blowing in the afternoon.

At about 6:30, Larry announced, "I think we should call it a night. Let's get our baths, fix something to eat and watch some cable."

Being so busy with the move, it seemed like ages since they had just sat down to relax. They hurried, Vanice to take a bath, Larry a shower, before they caught the film starting at 7 p.m.

Grabbing snacks, they settled down on the sofa in pajamas just as the movie *Crash* began.

Climbing into his patrol car, Rick Gregory then pulled onto Route 103 West, which ran straight as a chalk line through fallow cotton fields seven miles to the Mississippi River. He heard a fellow deputy on the radio calling Dispatch, asking if there were any warnings out yet. "Warnings" was the term that was used when radar readings indicated tornado conditions. No, Dispatch answered, no warnings yet.

Rick got on the radio and told the team, "I'm heading down to the Great River Road to watch." As he drove, Rick began to study the sky. He had never seen anything like it, never had such a ringside seat right on the edge of a super cell T-storm. It was as if the road was acting as a boundary.

The entire sky to the left, southward, was a pleasant, warm blue with golden sunlight. But everything to the north was a roiling, pitch-black mass of the meanest-looking cloud cover he'd ever seen. He pulled up at the intersection of 103 and Great River Road, and just sat and watched. Two ducks flew by, moving with the wind. To Rick it looked like they were going 100 miles an hour. He craned his neck out the car window and stared at the clouds. He could make out a distinct clockwise rotation taking shape.

Samantha Stanfield had been monitoring the weather reports all day. Her home was in Dyersburg, but her father, Joseph, Sr., 69, lived alone up on Harness Road in a place he'd spent his whole life. His wife and parents were buried in a little graveyard out back. Because it was east of a bluff, his house had always managed to avoid the strafing of storms.

Local lore held that tornadoes were forced to go around the bluff to the north or south. So whenever bad weather was afoot, Samantha and her husband would pack up the kids and drive the seven miles to ride out the storm at Poppy's. His house was the center for all family gatherings anyway. Holiday dinners, out-of-towners' visits, birthday parties—any special occasion would always be hosted at Poppy's. It was family headquarters. And Poppy's neighbors—Sid Bruce, Steve Harness, and the Taylors—had grown up together. They were as close as family.

But by early evening the reports coming in had Samantha concerned. Tornadoes had touched down in points that made a direct line toward Harness Road. When the sirens in Dyersburg went off, she called her father.

"Ah," Poppy said. "It'll never hit out here."

Then the line went dead. Samantha called him right back. It rang and rang. Finally he answered.

"Honey!" Poppy said, urgency in his voice. "I'm going to have to get off here! I think the roof's about to come off the house."

He screamed something she could not make out, and the line went dead again—for good.

Just fifteen minutes into *Crash*, Vanice and Larry Parker, sitting with the windows still open, heard click-click-clicking noises outside.

"It's hailing," Vanice said.

"Golly, it sure is," Larry said. Then they heard a roaring,

grinding sound like a huge cement truck backing toward the house.

"Is that a tornado?" Larry asked.

"It sounds like it."

"I don't know," Vanice said.

As they ran down the hall toward the west-facing bedroom, they saw it. Huge, dark, sucking up the earth and coming right for them. This wasn't any familiar funnel dancing across the landscape. It was an apocalyptic black curtain cutting off the sky, whipping round and round, snapping trees in half, tearing everything up.

They had nowhere to go, no basement, nowhere to hide. Larry tried pulling the mattress off the bed to cover them in the tub, but it was too heavy and he couldn't budge it. He and Vanice lay down side by side in the bathtub. She wrapped her arms around her husband. The porcelain was still wet from Vanice's bath.

The roar got louder. Louder than they thought noise could get. Their ears started popping as air being sucked into the vortex created a low-pressure zone. They could feel the whole house vibrating in their bones, shaking as violently as in an earthquake. Larry reached up and took hold of the faucet. He grasped it as if it were his last hold upon the earth. A split second later the lights went out.

"Hold on!" Larry yelled.

"Here it is!" After watching the monster tornado drop out of the clouds and head toward his home, Rick Gregory pushed the gas pedal to the floor.

"I've got to get home before it does," he said into the radio.

On his cell phone he told Laura, "It's on the ground. And I can't tell which way it's heading. Take cover!"

Racing alongside the cotton fields, he watched the quarter-mile-wide storm twist steel power-line towers like pretzels. Then the full force of the storm slammed into the bluff, bounced off, stalled, tried again, and a third time. It's trying to build steam to get over the bluff, he said to himself.

Finally, the massive cloud headed off to the left, away to the north and east. Sure that it had bypassed his house, Rick turned toward the bluff, chasing the vortex of wind. Already reports were coming in about homes damaged and people trapped. He headed up the road to the bluff, where he was stopped by a morass of huge, old trees. Uprooted, snapped and twisted apart, they blocked the narrow, winding road completely.

Rick got out of his car and started to run through the devastation. He had been up and down this road a thousand times— now he didn't recognize the area at all.

The Rev. Walter W. Asher of Christ United Methodist Church in Millsfield normally lets his Sunday evening service out promptly at 7 p.m. When folks emerged from the small 120-seat church on this Sunday evening, the sky to the west was very dark.

"You better stay here," one of his parishioners told him. "You don't want to be out there driving in that storm when it hits."

The Ashers lived twenty-five miles away to the north in Obion County, and it seemed unlikely the storm would strike that far north.

"Maybe I can beat it home," he said.

Rev. Asher and his wife left at about 7:20. They beat the worst of the storm, though they were hit with a good amount of hail, which was followed by a dead calm. But Asher was concerned about his congregation.

"Let's head back down that way and see what happened," he told his wife. As they turned around, his cell phone rang. It was one of his parishioners calling.

"They told me to tell you," she said. "The church is gone."

Downed trees were everywhere, and police were waving drivers away when Samantha got to within a quarter-mile of the turnoff to Poppy's.

There was a child trapped under a house, she was told, and they weren't letting anyone through. But she knew the back trails. She called a friend with access to a four-wheeler, and they pushed over the rutted paths toward Harness Road. Along the way, they passed people wandering in the opposite direction like dazed refugees trying to make their way out of a war zone.

Through the rain and darkness, Samantha could hear people screaming hysterically. Power lines were spitting sparks in the dark. The rain came down intermittently, cold and pitiless. Finally, even the four-wheeler could go no farther. Samantha and her friend got out and walked on, winding their way through a gnarled maze of downed trees.

When the tornado finally passed, Vanice and Larry Parker emerged from the bathtub and went to the living room. The furniture they'd been arranging and rearranging all day was piled in a heap in the dining room. Leaves and debris were scattered everywhere. Some of the screens on the open windows were blown in; others were blown out. Insulation had been sucked out of the wall, and ventilation ducts popped out of the floor. Somehow, though, their dream house had held together against the nightmare.

They were two of the lucky ones. Vanice opened the front door. A flash of lightning illuminated a ravaged battlefield: Two houses on the McAndrews' property directly across the street, the stone main house and a smaller frame structure, used by their college-age son and daughter, were gone, just gone. Vanice felt herself go limp as she dialed 911 on her cell phone.

"My neighbor's house has just been blown away by a tornado," she told the operator.

"Help is on the way," the dispatcher replied. Then Vanice's phone went dead.

She stepped back outside. That's when she saw the young people, the two McAndrew kids and three of their friends, screaming and crying, running from the rubble across the way. Oh, thank God they're alive, Vanice thought. But as the youngsters got closer, she saw terror in their eyes.

"Where's your mom?" she asked. "Where's your dad?"

They were out to dinner in town. The kids had been in the smaller house watching television when one of their parents called and warned them about the approaching tornado. The kids went outside, saw the storm towering across the sky, and had only seconds to run for cover in the basement of the stone house.

No sooner had they huddled together in one corner than the house was ripped apart. Shattered remnants collapsed into the basement, filling it with rubble. Only the spot where they hid was spared. The frame house where they had been and two more homes nearby were swept off the face of the earth.

The King and Hickman houses took a direct hit. The bodies of Janie King, a former teacher, and Travis Hickman, a retired lineman, were found that night. Eighty-seven-year-old Estelle Hickman, who lived with her son, was found the next morning. All three had been carried across a gully more than a quarter-mile away.

Walking through the war zone toward Poppy's place, Samantha had remained calm and determined, but when she finally came around the corner where she knew she should be able to see the house, she began freaking out.

All she saw were car lights shining on the barren side of the hill where Poppy's house should have been. She started to run. Poppy was sitting in the backseat of his car, all the windows busted out. He was dressed in white socks, white boxers and a white T-shirt, covered with blood and glass, holding an open umbrella, and trembling.

When Poppy had felt the roof coming off, he'd run for the bathroom in the center of the house. He got into the tub, but before he could slide the door shut, he knew that was it. He braced himself, closed his eyes, then felt himself sucked up into the air as the house blew apart above and around him.

What happened next is unclear. But when he opened his eyes, all he could see was a tangle of coat hangers. He groped his way out, pulling stuff off, and finally found himself lying on the lawn. His 3,200-square-foot split-level ranch house had vanished. The first thing Poppy did when he got to his feet was walk behind the foundation to make sure the tombstones of his wife and parents were still there. Then he came around to the front and saw that his car was parked on the concrete slab where his garage had been.

He climbed into the car, and smelled natural gas in the air. He was so muddled, he thought that starting the engine might trigger an explosion. So he put the car into neutral and pushed it back out of the garage area toward the street. And there he sat, with the headlights on, holding an umbrella to shield himself from the rain, glass all over him, a piece of wood stuck in his leg, a nail embedded in the back of his neck, trembling in the cold, not knowing what on earth to do but wait.

The house belonging to his neighbor, Sid Bruce, had been leveled. Sid's dog was hiding under the truck growling at anyone who came near.

Rick Gregory joined the rescue effort, and searchers found Mr. Bruce's body buried in the rubble. Steve Harness, in the home nearby, was okay, but in the next house down the road, Bill and Wanda Fay Taylor were not. That was the eeriest thing Rick had seen all night. The Taylors were found lying side by side, as if they had just gone to bed, right where the house had been, family photographs strewn around them.

On Biffle Road, east of Harness, there was another heartbreak. A young man and woman showed up and told people that their 11-month-old son had been in the house; the father's mother and stepfather were babysitting while the couple was having dinner in town. Volunteers searched. The bodies of all three were found in a field across the road.

It was about 2 a.m. before Patrolman Rick Gregory got home and collapsed into bed. His house had been untouched. The next day he was up early to take a look at the devastation from a helicopter. He had seen some wild stuff in his day, but this storm was in a class all its own.

The tornado was a category F3 storm with winds up to 200 miles per hour. It had been a half-mile wide, and carved an 18-mile-long path through Dyer County. In all, 24 lives were lost in Tennessee that evening, 16 of them in Dyer County and 8 in neighboring Gibson.

According to the Red Cross, 141 single-family homes were completely destroyed, and eighty homes sustained major damage, all in areas that were not densely populated. For the next week, it seemed like all Rick and his fellow deputies did was patrol Harness Road to keep looters and gawkers away, and to try to maintain some kind of order. After a couple of days, deputies were saying they'd had enough. They wanted duty in another part of the county.

Tales of amazing coincidence, heroism and heartbreaking tragedy gradually spread across the county.

There was the couple who survived when the husband lay on top of his wife holding her down on the floor while the wind pulled the rings off their fingers and the earrings from her ears.

The farmer whose 5,000-pound three-bottom breaking plow had been moved 300 yards.

A herd of miniature horses were found across the street from where they were penned—all survived save one.

At Rev. Asher's ruined church, the door of the mailbox had been ripped off, but the mail inside was undisturbed. A time capsule was found in the foundation of the church. It traced the history of the congregation back to 1904. Rev. Asher made photocopies and handed them out with song sheets (all the hymnals were lost) at Easter service, which was held at a nearby grammar school gym. Asher said they should make another time capsule for the new church, complete with copies of newspaper stories about the storm.

That Easter Sunday, Samantha Stanfield's young nieces wanted to do what they always did on Easter—go to Poppy's house. Even if there was no house. So they did. The entire family, including Poppy, drove up to Harness Road. Poppy talked about the trees, how all the big, pretty trees he had grown up around were gone. In his lifetime, he would never see them like that again. Samantha, at 32, knew that she probably would not either, though her kids might. The house was torn apart, but the family wasn't. The children celebrated Easter with an egg hunt on the foundation where Poppy's house once stood.

NIGHTMARE AT NAVAJO LAKE

BY DEREK BURNETT

This was Liz Marchand's summer to bond with her kids. She wanted to spend as many days with them as she could on Navajo Lake. The 36-year-old had left the insurance business to set up shop as a massage therapist in the resort town of Pagosa Springs, Colorado, where she lived with her husband, Mike, and four children—twins Mikaela and Maria, 7; her son, Austin, 6; and her stepdaughter, Marissa, 15.

Things had been rough lately for Marissa. Bright and with a flair for the dramatic, the teen had begun going through a period of rebellion. She started hanging with the wrong crowd, was charged with underage drinking and ended up performing community service at a local hospital. In the process, Marissa's relationship with her parents and Liz had suffered. Gradually, an uneasy truce had developed, and now she was feeling sheepish and scrutinized, and was looking for redemption.

Navajo Lake, 35 miles long, straddles the Colorado-New Mexico border. And it was the family's favorite recreation spot.

They'd been going there for more than a decade with friends to motorboat and camp.

Usually the Marchands went to the lake with their close friends the Mudrochs: Jim, Denise and their little boy, six-year-old Casey. This cloudy August 13, 2003, Liz was the only adult who could make it. With her were her four children, plus Casey, Marissa's 19-year-old friend Jenni, and the twins' friend Ivy, age 9.

At about 4 p.m., Liz chose a campsite 10 miles by boat from civilization and out of cell-phone range. They pitched their big blue dome tent in a wide, flat sandy area in a little cove. Liz and the older girls set heavy stones inside the tent to anchor it securely. Then they went motorboating and kneeboarding before settling down for dinner.

It had rained fitfully throughout the day, in little 15-minute bursts, but as night fell, Liz and the kids roasted marshmallows over the fire until a downpour drove them inside.

They had no inkling that miles away in the mountains, it was storming hard. Rain rushed through the washes, gathering force as gravity pulled it downhill until it became a debris-laden river where before there had been none.

Liz heard it coming—a runaway train in the wilderness—and knew what it was. She scrambled up, unzipped the door and bolted out of the tent as the water hit. "Marissa!" she screamed as cold water rushed over them and the tent began to turn on its base. "Jenni! Get out! Help me!"

The torrent pushed the tent full of kids toward the lake. Liz grabbed one of the fiberglass tent poles, and held on. Marissa and Jenni sprang through the door into the dark confusion of the sudden blast of water. They each grabbed poles and braced their feet in the silt to battle the current.

"Pull it to the left!" Liz shouted to the girls, spotting an area of higher ground a dozen feet away.

Slathered in wet mud, the three struggled together, but the stream was too much for them. It dragged the tent, now completely flattened, into the chest-deep water of the lake.

Inside, the children screamed and clung to air mattresses floating in the chaotic blackness of the tent's interior. One by one, they somehow escaped and were ushered by the girls onto dry land. All but one: little Casey, the Mudrochs' only child, who had zipped himself into a sleeping bag.

In a panic, Liz and the girls began plunging their arms into the tent, feeling for Casey. They pulled out sleeping bags, pillows, air mattresses, water jugs. No Casey.

Liz dived into the claustrophobic tangled mass searching for the boy. At last she touched something—the hair on his head. "I found him!" she blurted to the girls. Then she plunged back in, hauling up the impossibly heavy, waterlogged sleeping bag with the motionless child inside.

The girls helped her carry Casey to the shore, where the other kids were huddled and crying. "I think he's dead," Liz said in a hushed voice so the little ones couldn't hear. Yet without hesitation, she began CPR. Casey's little body was utterly still. No one was sure how long he had been underwater—five, ten minutes. He was cold, covered with mud, lifeless.

When she had come to the campsite, Liz had beached the boat and tied it off to some rocks a few feet from the tent. Now she looked up from doing CPR and saw the boat—their only link to civilization—drifting in debris-laden waters 60 feet away.

"Girls," Liz barked to Marissa and Jenni. "You have to take over CPR."

Jenni had been certified in the lifesaving technique two years earlier, and luckily Marissa had just completed a CPR course as part of her community service program.

The two girls took over from Liz; Marissa performed chest compressions while Jenni puffed breath between Casey's cold lips. His eyes and ears were filled with mud; filthy water spewed from his mouth with each compression. It was awful, gruesome work, but no one thought of quitting.

Liz considered swimming for the boat, and rejected the idea, certain she would drown in the flood if she tried. Then, a few feet away, she spotted an air mattress. She threw herself on it and paddled out to the boat.

The craft was caked in sludge, the engine clogged with mud. Without much faith, Liz turned the key. The motor caught and ran.

She had no spotlight, only the little red and green running lights, but she brought the boat around to the edge of the cove where the children were sobbing in the dark. One by one, she lifted them aboard. Marissa and Jenni carried Casey over the rocks and hauled him onto the boat. Once aboard, they crouched between the two captain's chairs and continued their grueling task: ten chest compressions, one breath. Repeat. Repeat. Repeat.

Earlier in the day, Liz had noticed a houseboat anchored directly across the lake about a mile away. Now she gunned the engine in that direction. Beyond the area affected by the flood, the lake was eerily calm and glasslike.

Once alongside the houseboat, Liz and the kids began screaming for help. A man and a woman stumbled out onto the deck.

Liz explained what had happened, and asked if the couple would take the four younger kids aboard and watch them while she went for help. They immediately agreed. Then, with the two girls still doing CPR on Casey's motionless form, Liz sped off.

It was ten miles to Arboles Marina, where there was a campground. By the running lights, Liz could see only a few feet in front of her, and went as fast as she dared. She steered by instinct and dead reckoning. There was a cell phone in the boat's glove compartment; she took it out and punched 911 again and again.

The girls were awfully quiet now, and Liz feared they were tiring or despairing. "Count the compressions!" she yelled to them. "Shout them out so I can hear them!"

For Marissa, calling out the compressions became a mantra. It helped dissolve her fears about the little boy she thought of as a brother. Yet how long could they keep breathing for him, keep his blood circulating?

Then a call went through. Liz stopped the boat dead in the water. "We need an ambulance at Arboles Marina. We're doing CPR on a six-year-old. He's not breathing." The phone disconnected. She had no idea if or how much of her message had gotten through. She hit redial and urged the boat forward.

The trip took on a heartbreaking repetition: The girls

chanted over the roar of the engine, and Liz redialed and redialed.

Another call went through. She slowed the boat. "We're on Navajo Lake . . ." The connection blinked off. Twice more this happened.

The girls were still counting out their chest compressions. Then suddenly they fell silent.

"What's going on?" Liz shouted.

"I think he's breathing."

Liz's heart leaped. "Don't stop," she said. The girls went back to their job.

Then out of the blackness, Liz saw something that made her almost queasy with relief: the lights of an emergency vehicle parked on the boat ramp at Arboles Marina.

She pulled up to the ramp, and two volunteer firefighters hefted Casey out of the boat. It had been more than an hour since the flood hit. By some miracle, Casey was breathing on his own when he was airlifted away.

The night had been brutally traumatic, and for Casey, the horrors were not to end soon. He spent 37 difficult days in a Denver hospital. There were touch-and-go moments, times when things looked hopeless again. But at every turn, his little body and big spirit prevailed. Today he is a healthy, active eight-year-old.

Dr. Alan Steinman, former chief medical officer for the U.S. Coast Guard, an expert on drowning, is not completely surprised that Casey survived without permanent impairment. "Children have a better survival rate than adults, especially in cold water," he says. "The heroic CPR provided his body with enough oxygen to spare him from irretrievable damage."

Sometimes crisis changes everything and everyone. At other times even traumatic events have no immediate or easily discernible effect. All the issues between Liz and Marissa were not resolved and their relationship was not magically transformed. There are still tensions between them, but each has a new respect for the other, and Marissa's life is back on track.

Life goes on. And that is enough. Just ask Casey.

LOST AT SEA

ANITA BARTHOLOMEW

Ben Pollock, his cousin Frank Doolin and their boys lazed on the deck of his 20-foot fishing boat. It had been one of the finest fishing days in memory—a fresh spring day in May 2004, during which they had caught a good 70 sea bass, groupers and grunts, enough to pack everyone's freezers.

The two men and their oldest sons, Gabriel Pollock and Michael Doolin, and another cousin, Jordan Stokes, had been out in the Gulf of Mexico since early morning, and now were enjoying the last warm rays of sunshine before turning back to port in Hudson, Florida. About 40 miles and two hours from shore, and an hour before sunset, they were looking forward to taking their catch home.

Pollock had recently bought the 1972-vintage craft and had taken it for a test run in the rougher waters of the Atlantic. Like most older boats, it had not been "foamed" (insulated with material to keep it buoyant if it capsized). Doolin had an uneasy feeling about this and told Pollock he wouldn't go out in an unfoamed vessel. But Pollock kidded with him until he relented.

Now as they turned off the reef, the boat seemed a bit sluggish. Pollock figured the hull had taken on some water. Easy to remedy. He pulled the plug from the hull to let gravity drain it as they motored back toward shore.

Several minutes later, the engine, out of gas, sputtered and died. Time to fill up from the spare tank.

Doolin had gotten little sleep the night before—an hour at best. But during that brief time, he'd had a nightmare. He dreamed about his son Michael—and in the dream Michael was drowning. It stayed with him, pricked his consciousness, as he headed to the back of the boat. Meanwhile, Pollock replaced the plug in the hull, grabbed the fuel and a funnel, and prepared to refill the side tank.

But now things were happening very quickly. The stern dipped low in the water. Waves began to wash over the sides. It felt like a hand was pushing the boat down. Doolin grabbed a five-gallon plastic bucket and began to bail. "Get the fuel in," he yelled.

Pollock bounded over. They dumped in the gas. Pollock frantically turned the key, trying to get the engine to crank. But it wouldn't catch—it was already underwater.

"Grab the life vests. Grab anything that will float!" Doolin called out. The boys jumped, and the men were flung into the water as the boat rolled.

Doolin gathered Michael, 13, and Jordan, 12, close to him as loose gear began popping up all around them. He took out his cell phone, which he kept in a plastic bag—and punched 911. Nothing. They were too far out.

"Get the rope," he yelled to Pollock. The anchor was pulling the boat down. And they would need the yellow plastic line. Pollock and Gabriel, the oldest boy at 14, sawed it off using the edge of the propeller. Then, balanced on the rocking, overturned boat, the younger two used it to tie themselves together.

"You boys just sit here," Doolin said, climbing aboard. "Don't let this thing tip over, because we might have to be out here all night." Outwardly the youngsters remained calm, but Doolin knew they must be terrified.

Pollock and Gabriel dove below to look for equipment and popped up in an air pocket—a pocket that reeked with gas fumes. Gabriel kicked his way back up and gathered life vests floating on the surface. While the others put the vests on, Pollock continued to dive, retrieving flares, a flashlight, a knife, an orange distress flag from inside the boat. He put these items into a small ice chest bobbing on the waves, and went down again.

Then came the hissing sound of escaping air. The boat was sinking. "Jump away, so it can't suck you under," Doolin yelled.

A moment later, the stern tipped downward; the bow pointed to the sky. Their largest ice chest, a king-sized white Igloo, about five feet long by three feet wide, was still tightly wedged between the steering column and the hull. It was packed with food and water, but was buoyant. They could use it to keep afloat. Pollock decided to risk one more dive.

He swam downward and grabbed the cooler's handle. It wouldn't budge. The sinking boat pulled him down with it, faster and faster. He yanked again, and it shot to the surface like a torpedo. Man and ice chest bounced out of the water.

"Whoo-hoo!" Pollock called jubilantly, swimming with the huge Igloo to the others. After donning a life jacket, he tied himself between his son and Jordan. Supplies were floating up all around them, and without thinking, Pollock opened another small cooler. Dozens of bloody fish spilled out. "Good grief, we're nothing but chum for the sharks," he cried. "We've got to get out of here. Swim!"

When they looked back from a hundred yards away, the boat was gone. The five of them were clinging to a bobbing ice chest in the open sea.

Pollock assured them help would come. Emulating his dad, Gabriel exuded bravado. "Man, this is nothing," he claimed. "The Marines do this all the time."

But Doolin knew the worst was still ahead. Within minutes, the gulf would swallow the big orange sun. No one could see them now. Nobody would be looking. Pollock had told their families that they might stay out an extra day—not to give it a thought if they didn't come home that night.

Temperatures fell. The gulf wind, soothing in the afternoon, sucked warmth from their bodies. Water temperatures in the 70s could bring on hypothermia within three hours. They shivered; their teeth chattered. And the fathers hugged the boys close.

It was about 10:15 p.m. A shrimp boat was speeding along a mile or so away. "Give me a flare!" Pollock shouted. On a night as dark as this, a flare would surely catch the eye of anyone on deck. He set it off, expecting a wide arc of flame. But the device barely flashed up an inch before dying.

"That was a flare?" Doolin said, half-laughing. Pollock popped a second. It shot up a bit higher, then fizzled. A third sputtered and flickered out, giving no more light than a matchstick. The flares he had retrieved were the oldest ones he'd had on board.

The flashlight! Its beam might be weaker, but would shine longer. Pollock rummaged through the small cooler where he had stowed salvaged items. Where was it? It had to be here. But it was gone. They all watched the shrimp boat disappear.

Every bone in Doolin's body was rattling. It would be so easy to give up now, to close his eyes and allow the sea to take him. But he had to stay in this for Michael.

A tall, thin boy, Michael had almost no body fat to insulate him from the cold. He was lethargic now, at times barely conscious. "Wake up, wake up," Doolin urged. The boy mumbled, and Doolin held him close, trying to forget the dream of the night before, praying that his son wouldn't die.

The other boys had also become weak and disoriented. Gabriel had the dry heaves from salt water he'd swallowed. His father cradled him, rubbed his arms to keep him warm. Jordan seemed to be hallucinating. The men couldn't understand what he was saying, but they understood his fear.

As dawn broke, Gabriel and Jordan perked up some. Michael was too weak to keep his head up. Doolin and Pollock tied him to the handle of the ice chest in order to keep his face out of the water. They had been adrift for almost 12 hours with no relief from the cold. It would be hours still before the sun warmed the air and sea.

They swam east toward the shore. Jellyfish stung their legs, but they pushed on. By 7 a.m., staring at the vast emptiness, Pollock felt despair. Where were all the boats? They had been an hour from shore when their own went down. They should be seeing fishing vessels out on the water soon. But would the boats see them?

Doolin understood that nobody was going to spot five heads bobbing just above the water. He had fished the Florida Keys and knew that fishermen looked for diving frigate birds to point them to fish. What could they toss in the air that would resemble a bird diving for prey? They had the small white cooler—that would have to do.

Sometime past eight o'clock, two boats appeared, far southwest of them. Doolin threw the little cooler into the air. Pollock tossed their distress flag. Gabriel and Jordan joined in, shouting, yelling, throwing whatever they could. The boats sped past.

Doolin took a close look at Michael. He was as limp as a dishrag, barely conscious, no longer even trembling. Haunted by his dream, Doolin blamed himself for bringing his boy fishing, and for their predicament.

Joe Miley, James Fullerton and his wife, Carol, were headed to a fishing hole 35 miles out from Hudson. With Miley at the wheel, *InTheCooler* sped along at 24 knots. After more than an hour pounding over the waves, Miley stopped to give them all a break. Idling, the boat acted like it had picked up some sea grass. As Miley checked the prop, the boat drifted south.

When he finished, he glanced to the horizon. Something was moving. It was just a speck. Birds diving, or maybe sea turtles. That could mean a reef. And reefs meant fish. "You mind if we go downrange a couple of miles?" he asked Fullerton.

Fullerton was reluctant. "Man, we've got a ways to go."

But, if they found fish, Miley said, they wouldn't have to go any farther. They decided to check it out.

Drawing closer, the movement looked more like debris floating on the water than birds or turtles. But Miley pushed on. Maybe that white thing hopping up and down in the air was a bird after all.

Closer still, and he thought for a second that it looked like people out there. But it couldn't be. "Oh, my God," cried Carol Fullerton. "There are children in the water." Now they could hear shouting and yelling.

Tears welled up in Doolin's eyes as the boat pulled alongside them. The people on deck helped get Michael and the other two kids into the boat. Then he and Pollock climbed aboard. A woman wrapped his son in blankets and towels, while the men powered the boat toward shore.

Over and over, Doolin, Pollock and the boys thanked their rescuers.

What to make of Doolin's dream? Was it a premonition? Coincidence? What we do know is that Michael and the others survived, healthy and with no lasting effects. We know that they all owe their lives to a big cooler that kept them afloat, a little cooler that flew like a bird, and three fishermen aboard *InTheCooler* who found them adrift in the open sea.

BURIED ALIVE!

BY BETH MULLALLY

Eugene Zerbe chipped ice off his windshield while his '86 Chevy Cavalier was warming up in the parking lot of the P. J. Valves Company in Myerstown, Pennsylvania. It was the fifteenth major storm of the season, and the heavy snow was mixing with sleet.

When Zerbe, a machinist, had punched out a few minutes earlier, his timecard said 4:31 p.m., Wednesday, March 2, 1994. His wife, Sandra, would be putting supper on the table at 5:30, as she did every evening.

In the nearly thirty years he'd been commuting over Blue Mountain to his home in Pine Grove, Pennsylvania, Zerbe, 57, had never seen a winter like this. Rather than take his usual shortcut home over a rural country road, he decided to make the twenty-mile trip over the 1450-foot mountain on the well-traveled Route 501.

Driven by 50-m.p.h. winds, the sleet was getting worse as he turned onto 501 north. As Zerbe crept along the slippery road

toward the mountain, ice thickened on his windshield. He was
not alarmed—driving in snow and ice had become routine this
winter—but it struck him as odd that no cars were coming
from the opposite direction.

It took a half-hour to travel the five miles to the flat stretch
of road leading to the base of the mountain. Here the highway
opened up, and wide-open fields flanked either side. He suddenly understood why he had seen no cars in the southbound
lane—already, ice-encrusted drifts buried the road under two
feet of snow. He began to notice trapped cars on both sides of
the road.

Suddenly Zerbe's blue Chevy came to a dead stop, caught
fender-deep in a drift. His tires spun futilely. He tried rocking
the car back and forth between forward and reverse. It wouldn't
budge.

Sandra Zerbe checked the turkey roasting in the oven, then
looked out the window at the snow, thinking of Eugene. From
the moment she first saw him, she knew he was the man she
would marry. When she moved to Pine Grove as a teen-ager,
she noticed that he and his friends had a favorite street corner.
She'd stroll by, hoping the handsome, dark-haired fellow would
notice her. Eventually he did.

Now, married thirty-five years, she and Eugene had raised
four children—Kim, Tim, Jim and Eugene II ("Chuck")—who
were all grown with families of their own. As Sandra waited,
Kim, who lived nearby, appeared at the door.

"I'm sure he's okay," Sandra told her. The two women took
turns telling each other there was nothing to worry about.

Dressed only in coveralls, sneakers, and his medium-weight work jacket, Zerbe got out of his car to begin chipping away at the ice. He quickly realized he had made a mistake. Stunned by the wind's force, he had to hold on to the door with his un-gloved hands to remain upright. The freezing pellets stung his skin and soaked his clothing, plastering his coveralls to his legs and weighing down his jacket.

Retreating inside, he watched the storm with growing anxi-ety. The snow was building so rapidly that in only fifteen min-utes a drift piled up above the top of the window.

A half-hour later, he heard snowmobile engines. Soon a face covered by a ski mask peered in his window. "Any women or children in there with you?" the snowmobiler asked. He and five others had been called out to evacuate stranded motorists, women and children first.

"I'm alone," Zerbe replied. "I'm okay—just wet and cold."

"There's a front-end loader up ahead pulling cars out of the drift," the snowmobiler said. "He'll be along for you. Just sit tight."

Over three miles away, Dave Bernhard, the road-crew foreman, watched as the operator of a front-end loader tried to work the machine into the drift. In his fifteen years with the state De-partment of Transportation, he had never seen snow pile up so quickly. In only a few minutes it had drifted to a depth of six feet, covering all but the radio antennas of cars stranded on the highway. Plows were useless.

Riding on top of the drifts, the snowmobilers eventually evacuated seventy people from their cars. They believed they had got everyone, and had—except Zerbe. When they returned to his stretch of the road, they saw nothing but snow and left the scene. No one imagined that a man was entombed beneath the ice-encrusted snow.

Kim called the state police every half-hour. Each time the dispatcher told her, "No word yet. If anyone spots his car we'll let you know."

Finally, at midnight, the dispatcher had some news. A four-mile section of Route 501 had been closed due to drifting. Motorists were being evacuated, and the Mount Aetna firehouse was being set up as an emergency shelter.

Kim and her mother breathed small sighs of relief. Yet they thought it was strange that Eugene hadn't called to say he was all right. Sandra sent her daughter home at 2 a.m. with a promise to call the minute she had word. She read the Bible for a few minutes, then lay down to sleep.

Zerbe pulled his mini-flashlight out of his pocket to check the time—2:15 a.m. It had been a while since he'd heard snowmobiles.

He was tempted to get out of the car again, but his wet clothes were a reminder that he'd accomplished nothing the first time. And by now a mountain of snow was leaning in on his car door.

His body began to tremble with cold, his hands shaking so badly he had trouble putting the key in the ignition. He couldn't leave the car running for long, as the fuel gauge showed nearly empty, but he wanted the heat on for a few minutes so he would stop shivering.

Zerbe shut down the engine and leaned back in his seat. *They'll come back for me,* he told himself, drifting off to sleep.

By 7:30 a.m., despite the raging storm, Sandra's house was filled with concerned relatives.

"We're going to find him," Tim said. Knowing no ordinary vehicle would make the trip, he had an idea: Since both he and Chuck were members of the National Guard, they could borrow one of its trucks.

Bundled against the weather, Tim and Chuck walked to the local armory and clambered into an Army truck. By 9:30 they had picked up Kim and Jim and were heading south on Route 501 toward Blue Mountain. They soon found themselves in an eerie, wintry wasteland, where visibility was only a few feet.

Inching their way along at five m.p.h., the Zerbes took two hours to travel ten miles up the mountain and down the other side. As they continued another mile south, they approached the northern edge of the drift. It looked like the wall of a glacier.

A state policeman flagged the truck down. "This is as far as you're going," he told them. "There's no way to get through for the next four miles." A front-end loader at the edge of the drift, scooping snow a bucketful at a time, was making scant progress.

"How soon before we'll be able to get through here?" Tim asked.

"Maybe by Saturday," the trooper replied.

Two days! What if Dad was somewhere in that drift?

"We'll go around," Kim said.

Tim turned the truck and inched back on 501 heading

north. Before reaching the mountain, he turned onto another route leading to Myerstown so he could pick up 501 on the other side of the drift and retrace the route he believed his father had taken. But the truck reached another wall of snow.

Kim was overcome with despair. "How are we ever going to get to him?" she whispered.

"We'll walk," said Chuck. With less blowing snow and clearer visibility, he and Jim got out of the truck and groped their way to the top of the drift. Snow was piled halfway up telephone poles, and there was no other sign that this had ever been a road. In the distance they saw a snowmobile heading their way.

Dale Swope had been working much of the night, shuttling people from their cars to the Mount Aetna firehouse. "There's no one out there," Swope told the Zerbes when he approached them. "Your father's got to be on some other road."

Devastated, the Zerbes headed home. For the first time, Kim began to wonder if her father was still alive.

Not two thousand feet away from where Chuck and Jim had stood, Zerbe sat buried in his car. *Got to warm up,* he thought, surprised at how slowly his fingers responded when he moved them toward the ignition key. The trembling had stopped during the night, but now a deep numbness had overtaken him. Finally he turned his wrist and the engine came to life. Zerbe sat back while the car warmed up.

He felt groggy and disoriented, as if he'd been drugged. Only gradually did he notice the smell. *Exhaust fumes! The pipe must be iced over. I could die of carbon-monoxide poisoning!*

He shut off the engine, then groped clumsily for the window

crank. Only as he rolled down the window did Zerbe realize to his horror that his entire car was encased in ice.

Panicking, Zerbe clawed and pounded at the sharp, jagged snow. *I have to get air,* he thought frantically. Groping beneath the seats, he discovered an ice scraper. Panting with exertion and fear, he began chipping his way upward inch by inch, ice flying in his face. Finally he broke through to the surface, the tiniest of holes in his icy tomb.

He leaned back, laughing, and breathed deeply of the fresh air. But his exhilaration was short-lived. He could sense the air growing colder as the biting wind snaked downward through the opening. His clothes, still wet from the night before, began to freeze on his body. *I could die of hypothermia,* he thought.

With the cold overtaking his body, Zerbe sank deeper into reverie. He knew there was nothing more he could do. *Please help me, God,* he prayed.

As Zerbe's body temperature began to decrease, blood flow to his extremities slowed, leaving them numb, while the flow remained strong throughout his midsection to protect his vital organs from the assault of the cold. His heart rate and respiration slowed and his blood pressure plummeted. Slowly, he faded into unconsciousness. And, gradually, Zerbe's body temperature dropped toward death.

Sandra sent her relatives home before midnight. By now Eugene had been missing for thirty-two hours. She spent the night sleepless, curled on the couch, begging God to bring her husband home to her.

Shortly after 8 a.m. on Friday, road crews began marking

the presence of buried cars with orange traffic cones. As Dave Bernhard trudged through what appeared to be an empty expanse of snow, he spotted a small hole. He knelt down to peer in, and to his surprise he discovered another car.

Scooping away snow, he cleared a large enough space so he could press his face against the car window. Inside, an ashen-faced man was leaning back in the driver's seat. His eyes were rolled back into his head. At first Bernhard suspected the man was dead, but then he saw his head move slightly. "Hey!" Bernhard shouted. "Can you hear me? Hang on!" There was no answer.

Bernhard scrambled over to the loader working nearby. "I found someone buried in a car!" he shouted. Instructing the loader operator to start digging, Bernhard went to his truck and radioed for help. Then he grabbed two shovels and ran back.

The loader lumbered over, and the driver began digging, slowly exposing the blue car. Other rescuers arrived by snow-mobile, and several men jumped down into the cleared hole to help dig the last foot out by hand. "We're here to help you!" they shouted to the unconscious man inside.

After twenty-five minutes rescuers cleared the driver's door of snow, but it wouldn't open. Peering in the window, Bernhard saw that it was locked. And with Zerbe slumped behind the wheel, the rescuers didn't dare break the window.

Since they had removed enough snow from the left rear window, they broke through it. The loader operator reached in and opened the front-door lock. It was 9 a.m. Zerbe had been trapped inside the car for forty hours.

Pulling Zerbe from the car, the rescuers hoisted him over

their heads to others at the top, who laid him in the snowmobile driven by Dale Swope. "Let's go!" shouted Swope, noticing that Zerbe's legs were stiffened in position, and his socks were frozen to his legs.

Zerbe was delivered to the firehouse within fifteen minutes. His frozen clothing was removed, his body surrounded with warm packs, and warm fluids were pumped through a needle inserted in his arm. His temperature had dropped to near 85 degrees, less than two degrees from probable death.

Zerbe responded swiftly. His heart rate returned to normal and his blood pressure rose. His breathing became deeper and more regular. Soon his face took on color and life.

Finally Zerbe opened his eyes and looked at the crowd of worried faces around him. "You're going to be okay, Mr. Zerbe," a paramedic reassured him. "We're taking you to the hospital." But Zerbe didn't say anything—he couldn't remember how to form words. Soon a helicopter flew him to Hershey Medical Center, thirty miles away.

By the time his family joined him in the emergency room an hour later, Zerbe was showing small signs of recovery. Sandra and their four children stood tense and silent while Dr. John Field tested his mental state.

"Can you tell me your name?" the doctor asked.

After a long pause, Zerbe finally spoke. "I'm Eugene Zerbe."

To the amazement of the hospital staff, Zerbe would be declared fully recovered and sent home three days later. Dr. Field agreed that medical science alone could not explain Zerbe's incredible survival. "Faith was at work here," Sandra Zerbe declared.

TRAPPED BY A KILLER FIRESTORM

BY MARK STUART GILL

In the Los Angeles suburb of Malibu, 17-year-old Eddie Bedrosian sat fooling around with his electric guitar. His high school had been let out early that morning of November 2, 1993, because of brush fires in the area.

Glancing out the window, Eddie saw fiery clouds rising from the mountains to the east. *Another brush fire*, he thought. *No need to worry.* His home on Sierks Way had always been protected by stiff breezes that blow off the Pacific, less than a quarter-mile away.

The tall, skinny senior was more concerned about the essay he had to write about himself for his college application. It should have been finished weeks before. *I've never done anything worth writing about*, he thought. *They'll think I'm a nobody.*

In his head, he could hear his mother, Pat Bedrosian, lecturing him: *Why aren't you working on your essay? You've got to stop procrastinating. Do I have to get your grandmother in here to talk to you?*

Eddie cringed. He knew how much his grandmother, Hazel Bedrosian, wanted him to go to college. "Education is the key to everything in America," she had always said. When Eddie was much younger, she'd told him the story of how she escaped from Armenia and came to the United States.

"It was 1915," she said. "I was a teenager when the Turks stormed into our village and started to burn houses. They killed my father and brothers. I escaped with nothing." Tears sprang from her eyes.

"Don't cry," little Eddie said, hugging her.

"When I came to America," Hazel continued, "I saw the dreams come true for people who worked hard and learned. I had two children and a full-time job, but I became the first person in my family to earn a high-school diploma."

No matter how many times Eddie heard the story over the years, it always touched his heart.

In the family room down the hall, 93-year-old Hazel Bedrosian sat on the couch. Still independent, she lived in her own apartment nearby, but she liked spending time with the family. Her eyes were glued to the television set. "Bigger and more dangerous than anything in a quarter-century," an announcer said. "Seven thousand firefighters can't control them. The steep hillsides of Malibu are tinder-dry from seven years of drought."

Hazel smelled burning piñon trees, turned off the TV, and shuffled outside. Marc Winnikoff, a 35-year-old architect who lived across from the Bedrosians, was hosing down his roof with the help of a friend, Renato Vasquez.

The Bedrosian ranch house was on the south side of Sierks Way, a remote hillside cul-de-sac that runs east to west along a ridge overlooking deep canyons to the north and south. Shortly after 1 p.m., a firetruck drove across the bottom of the north canyon. "Stay calm," a voice boomed up from a bullhorn. "We will advise you if you need to evacuate."

Pat dumped drawers full of bank and insurance papers in the trunk of her white Lincoln Continental. "Eddie, I don't know how much time we've got," she said. "We have to take as many things as we can."

Eddie grabbed the remote control to watch the news. The TV was dead.

His heart began to race. He picked up the phone to call his father, who was in Washington, D.C., on business, but the line was also dead.

"Eddie, hose down the roof," his mother shouted from the next room.

He grabbed a garden hose and climbed a ladder. Straddling the peak of the roof, black smoke stinging his eyes, Eddie sprayed water over the wood shingles. He looked down and saw his grandmother shuffling nervously in the driveway.

By the time he reached the ground, his mother still wasn't finished packing. But she was deeply anxious about her son and her mother-in-law.

"You've got to get your grandmother out of here," she said. Then she locked eyes with him. "Eddie," she added, "you are your grandmother's protector for the rest of the day."

A mile away, the blaze was sucking in the air, superheating it to over 2000 degrees Fahrenheit and exploding it upward into tornado-force whirlwinds. The fire devoured everything in its path.

High above the flames, planes dropped fire-retardant chemicals, and helicopters dumped 3000-pound loads of seawater onto the blazing shoulders of the inferno. But like an enraged monster, the jagged orange line of fire pushed ahead.

Hazel Bedrosian shivered with fear on the patio. Her fingers tore at her thin white hair as 80-year-old memories flooded into her head. *The Turks are burning everything. They'll kill you if you stay, Mama. Get up* . . . She gasped for air and clutched at her chest in pain. Eddie put a wet handkerchief to her face. He felt it was time to get out of there. Even if his mother was taking the car, the quickest way out, it seemed to him, was to hike down the north hillside, which led to the Pacific Coast Highway. Eddied guided his grandmother into the back yard, and they started to descend the 45-degree slope.

Suddenly, they heard a whooshing rumble. It was the sound of the fire, howling like an approaching freight train.

Hazel shrieked and jerked away from Eddie. Losing her balance, she fell and began to slide. Instantly, Eddie scrambled after her, grabbing her before she disappeared into the brush.

At the same moment, Eddie saw a raging mass of orange fire boil over the opposite rim of the canyon two hundred yards away. The heat scorched his face.

They were less than one hundred yards from the bottom of the canyon now, and Eddie could make out the Pacific Coast Highway. But with a sick feeling, he realized that the fire racing down the opposite hill would reach the bottom before they did. He might be able to make it on his own, but not with his grandmother.

"Grandma, we've got to go back," he screamed, pulling Hazel up the slope.

"Down. We have to go down," she said, tugging her hand away defiantly.

Currents of fire had already traveled across the bottom of the canyon and were slicing up the hill toward them. Eddie couldn't argue anymore. "Move, Hazel Bedrosian!" he shouted in an authoritative voice he had never used before.

With his hands under her armpits, Eddie pulled his grandmother back up the hill. The pursuing fire howled in his ears, spitting ashes so thick he could taste the acrid grit on his lips.

They staggered the last few feet to their yard and into the middle of Sierks Way, where they sat down to catch their breath. The fire crested over the top of the hill forty yards behind their house. But now another fire leapt off the hills from the east and was only one hundred yards away, at the entrance to Sierks Way. *This is it*, Eddie thought. *We're going to die.*

"Eddie!" It was Winnikoff. He and Vasquez had heard from a neighbor that the road was cut off. "We've got to find a way out!" he said.

"Maybe we could climb down behind your house," Eddie said, looking toward the south side of the canyon.

"It's a complete jungle back there," Winnikoff said. "I don't know my way."

"What are we going to do?" Hazel moaned.

"We've got to find a way down the south slope," Eddie said. "It's our only chance."

Along the winding road that led out of the canyon, Pat Bedrosian kept looking out her rear-view mirror. She thought Eddie had taken Hazel and left with neighbors in their car. *They must be right behind me,* she told herself, *unless they already got out.* Carefully, she maneuvered around downed electrical wires.

Suddenly, she slammed on the brakes. A fire vehicle in front of her had gotten hung up on a log that had rolled in its path. A man slid into the driver's seat of Pat's car. "We've got to clear the road," he said. "We're right in the path of the fire." He nudged the Lincoln into the back of the fire vehicle, revved the engine in neutral, then slammed the lever into drive. The wheels screeched as the Lincoln shot forward, pushing the vehicle from the log.

In under a minute, they were safely on the Pacific Coast Highway. There was no sign of Eddie. *My God! Eddie and Hazel!* Pat thought. *Where are they?*

On the south slope, Vasquez swung a machete in mighty arcs, hacking a path down the canyon. Eddie and Winnikoff followed a few yards behind, dragging Hazel, her arms around their necks. She was breathing in labored gasps. *Is she having a heart attack?* Eddie wondered.

The trail Vasquez was forging grew more treacherous. Ten yards to the right was a sheer drop. Eddie moved left and, nearly blinded by the smoke, almost stepped off a cliff.

He could hear mesquite trees exploding like cherry bombs from their own boiling resin. His throat was so dry he could barely speak, and his lungs were burning. But he had to keep going.

From out of the smoke, a cloud of hot embers dropped on them like angry bees. They sat Hazel down, and Eddie arched his body over hers, trying to shield her. The searing embers bit at his neck and arms.

Animals were shrieking in terror and agony. A wild-eyed deer barreled past; a bird hopped along pathetically.

"Go without me," Hazel said, curling up on the ground. "Save yourself."

"Let's move it!" Eddie heard Winnikoff yell. "The fire must be right on our heels."

"C'mon Grandma, we're going to survive this." He and Winnikoff reached down and picked her up like a child.

Eddied had no idea if the Pacific Coast Highway at the bottom of the canyon was a foot away or hundreds of yards. All he knew was that if he stopped, he might never be able to start again. He and Winnikoff lunged forward together, carrying Hazel. Ten yards, fifteen yards. Eddie's arms were going into spasm.

Smoke billowed heavily as they struggled forward. Thirty yards, thirty-five yards. Then Eddie's sneakers struck hard ground, and he heard Winnikoff shouting, "We're alive!"

Two firefighters ran toward them. Paramedics assisted Hazel with respirators and an automatic defibrillator. Eddie felt dizzy and nauseated.

"Where did you come from, kid?" a paramedic asked as he worked.

"There," gasped Eddie hoarsely, pointing. The dry grass they had just struggled through was ablaze.

The fireman looked back at Eddie with disbelief. "You just walked through hell and lived."

It was 7 p.m. Pat Bedrosian sat on a folding chair in a temporary shelter at the Malibu Community Center. She couldn't eat, and the chill inside her wouldn't go away. *Where's my family? Have I lost my son? Have I lost Hazel?* she thought.

Night fell. Pat cried herself into an uneasy sleep. A couple of hours later, someone woke her, calling her to the phone. "Mom!" said the voice on the other end.

"Eddie!" she cried. "You're alive! Where's your grandmother?"

"She's okay. Only some cuts and smoke inhalation. She's with me."

Pat spoke to her son through tears of joy. "You've saved her life," she said.

He smiled. Now he had something to write his college essay about.

THE TOT AND THE TWISTER

BY DEREK BURNETT

On April 3, 2012, in the Diamond Creek subdivision of For-ney, Texas, the Enochs family awoke to an ordinary day. Sherry Enochs, 52, saw her husband, Mike, off to his job in nearby Dallas and her 15-year-old son, Denver, off to school. Then she opened the doors of her at-home day care to the two small children she would be watching that day. At around 11:30, Sherry's daughter Lindsey, 22, kissed her 19-month-old son, Laine, left him in her mother's care, and hurried off to her own day care job.

Quiet, strong, and compassionate, Sherry Enochs had spent her life taking care of everyone. She had raised five children of her own and was a doting grandmother. Today, in addition to Laine and the two children she was watching—19-month-old Abigail and three-year-old Connor—the house was home to two dogs (a Pekingese and an ancient two-pound Chihuahua), a mother cat with a newborn litter of kittens in a playpen in the bedroom, and a couple of goldfish.

Around midday, she got a call from her daughter Megan, 26, who was five months pregnant and living about seven miles away in Heartland. "Look at the TV, Mom," she said.

On-screen, news crews were showing footage from Lancaster, just 30 miles away, of a tornado hurling tractor-trailers around.

"Is it coming this way?" asked Sherry.

"No. It sounds like it's going to stay west of Forney."

Relieved, Sherry turned her attention back to the children, busying herself to such an extent that she never heard the sirens warning residents to seek shelter. Laine was in his toddler bed watching a cartoon. Connor and Abigail were playing on the floor. Then Sherry's cell rang: Megan again.

"Mom, look outside!" This time, there was a note of urgency in her voice.

Sherry went down the hallway to her bedroom. She looked out the window, and her heart lodged in her throat. A tornado was tearing across the open field adjacent to the subdivision. It was massive—a great vaporous funnel with a dogleg bend in it tapering down to an earthward point all the more menacing for its slender, stylus-like precision. Behind it the sky was black, and at its edges bits of debris were churning as it passed over businesses across the way. Was that the dry cleaner's? she thought. A jagged bolt of lightning fired inside the funnel. The twister's path was now obvious: It was heading right into Diamond Creek.

"It's here, Megan," Sherry yelled. "The tornado is here!"

Keeping Megan on the phone, she ran down the hall to the front room. There she scooped up Laine and Abigail and hustled Connor back up the hallway and into the middle bathroom. "Get in the tub," she ordered the bewildered kids. The Enochses had no cellar, so the tub would be the safest place to take cover.

She climbed into the bathtub and sat Abigail and Connor

shoulder-to-shoulder, placing her legs over them. She felt confident they'd stay still, but Laine was panicking, so she clutched him in her lap facing her.

Through the phone Megan heard the roar of the tornado and something else she'd never heard before: Her mother screaming. Then the phone went dead.

"Mom? Mom!"

For two minutes, Megan called her mother's name. Then she sank to her knees, sobbing.

At 2:00, Lindsey and her colleagues at the day care center got the word to take the children to the building's "weather areas" (central, windowless rooms). Once she had her kids tucked away safely, she stepped out into the hallway where her bosses were talking about the situation. "Diamond Creek has been hit," one of them said.

Horrified, Lindsey called her mother. Nothing.

Sherry had expected the tornado to sound like a freight train. That's what everyone compares it to. But freight trains do not drown out the whole world. There had been an eerie quiet, and then the house's electrical system had shut down with an audible pop. And soon the winds were so violent that she couldn't hear her own screams. The tornado even drowned out the sound of its own destruction: no crashing of shattering glass, no moaning of splintering boards—only the hellish, booming roar of 150 mph winds. But whether or not Sherry could hear it, the twister was laying waste to her home. Observers watched as the house seemed to explode into the tornado as if struck by a bomb, turning the funnel from grayish-white to deep brown as it sucked building materials and the family's belongings up from the ground.

And then the tornado tried to snatch up Laine. Sherry clutched at her grandson for all she was worth, so much so that she never noticed the broken-off boards with exposed nails slamming into her head, shoulders, back, and ribs, puncturing her skin and leaving bloody holes surrounded by great yellow bruises. She also had no idea that she was no longer in the bathtub. Somehow, the twister had lifted her and the three children free, spilling them into the wind. And now Laine was sliding away from her.

"Megan, have you talked to Mom? Are they OK?" It was Lindsey calling.

Megan was crying. "I don't know!"

"What do you mean?"

"I don't know. I don't know." That's all she could say.

Ignoring her boss's pleas to stay put, Lindsey jumped into her car and sped through the empty streets of Forney, squinting through a rain-streaked windshield. The roads were clear until she approached Diamond Creek, where a logjam of emergency vehicles brought her progress to a halt.

Sherry grabbed Laine's chubby legs above the ankles and strained to pull him back against her. She felt the little boy slipping and applied all her strength to the fearsome tug-of-war she was waging with the tornado.

I'm doing what I can, she thought, but I don't know if it's enough. The storm suddenly sucked harder, nearly yanking the boy free, and Sherry bore down, fighting back with the last of her energy. "I'm losing him!"

And then the tornado moved on. The battle was over. The struggle to save Laine had lasted somewhere between four and ten seconds.

As soon as the tornado left Diamond Creek, the subdivision began to fill with police, firefighters, and Good Samaritans. The air hissed with gas from sheared-off piping, and police officers tried to keep civilians away from the homes. An officer shouted to one neighbor to get away from Sherry's house, but he waved him off, yelling, "There are people in there!"

Dazed, Sherry looked around. Laine was on her lap, shaken and crying. His mouth and nose were filled with mud and insulation, but he was unhurt, aside from a scratch on his arm. But there was no sign of Connor or Abigail. She tried to look for them, but she could not stand up. Spotting the neighbor, she called out for help.

"I'll get you out, as soon as I can get through this debris."

Debris? Then it hit her: She shouldn't be able to see him. There were no windows in the middle bathroom. In fact, where *was* the middle bathroom? Looking about, she realized that she was in the open air, trapped in a small hole, up to her neck in wreckage. As the neighbor worked to free her, others rushed onto the scene. "There are two more kids," Sherry said, passing Laine through the hole.

When they got her clear, she stood in her flip-flops with Laine in her arms, gaping at what, minutes earlier, had been her home. Nothing was intact except the master bathroom, where a four-foot piece of wall still stood with a crooked pipe and piece of board forming a weird cross at its top. Otherwise, the building was entirely flattened; she could look right over what was left of her house into the backyard. And what she saw there was three-year-old Connor, barefoot among the broken glass and wind-scattered nails, wandering soberly through the debris with no greater injury than a scrape on his head. A police officer scooped him up and carried him to his car.

"There's one more," Sherry yelled.

The police officer rushed back to the flattened house, two steps behind one of Sherry's neighbors, who was following the sounds of a small child's cries. They found Abigail where two walls had collapsed together leaving a tiny void, and they lifted her out of the rubble. She was scraped and bruised but not seriously injured.

Lindsey counted the houses on her mother's street. The fourth house—Sherry's—was nothing but an ugly pile of wood and glass and shingles. She felt the life drain out of her. Somewhere in all that mess, she assumed, lay the lifeless bodies of her mother and son. The police were telling her she couldn't get any closer to the house, so she jumped the curb and parked in the grass, then ran through the field, losing her shoes in the mud. A firefighter stopped her.

"My mom and my baby. They were in here," she yelled.

"The grandma and the baby?"

Lindsey burst through a neighbor's door. There was her mother sitting on the couch, battered and bloodied, holding a muck-covered Laine. A thousand emotions washed over Lindsey. Horror and dread and relief and disbelief had all combined to reduce her to a kind of animal fury. As another sister, Ashley, took a step toward her, Lindsey inexplicably took a swing at her. She pounded on Ashley until she was pulled off, and she came to her senses. Sobbing, she enveloped Laine in her arms, then hugged her mother, repeating, "I'm sorry, Mom. I'm so sorry."

The tornado that destroyed the Enochs home destroyed 73 homes in Diamond Creek, even while some nearby homes were barely touched. Thankfully, there were no fatalities.

Sherry has recovered physically, but emotionally it's been hard. "We lost everything," she says. "I'll have a little meltdown every so often. I'll just start crying."

Laine refused to enter a bathtub for a week after the storm but now appears unfazed by the event. Mostly the family is just grateful and incredulous that their loved ones were spared. After the tornado, they found their tiny 14-year-old Chihuahua, Bella, alive and still in her crate, which had landed in the driveway. Their Pekingese and all the kittens and their mother survived unscathed. Only the goldfish perished.

Most of the family's belongings were smashed or disappeared, with no pattern to what was spared. Sherry's collection of glass angels survived intact. And Laine's lightweight toddler bed never budged, although every adult bed in the house was lost.

No one knows how Connor ended up in the backyard or how Abigail came to be found down the hallway from the bathroom where they had taken shelter. Tim Marshall, a meteorologist, says it's not uncommon for groups of people caught in twisters to end up in different places and to not know how they got there. "When you're in a tornado, it's a fog of rotating debris, with zero visibility," he says. Factor in the overwhelming noise, and it's easy to see how anyone would become completely disoriented. Still, Sherry is mystified: The bathtub in which she'd taken shelter was nowhere to be found. It had vanished, blown off to parts unknown.

The family lived with Megan until a new home was built just a stone's throw from the ruins of their old place. Every day, Lindsey thinks about how her mother never let go of Laine. "It doesn't surprise me, though," she says. "My mother would do anything to protect a child. Anything."

AGAINST THE SEA

BY MALCOLM McCONNELL

The 30-foot fiberglass boat pitched on the sunlit sea as Vivienne Slear, 44, adjusted her face mask. "Remember to stay together down there," dive master Kevin Frank warned. The eight scuba enthusiasts were about to explore a coral reef between Goat Island and Little Tobago, a pair of tiny islets less than two miles off the northeast coast of Tobago in the West Indies. Frank would be dragging a weighty spool attached to a buoy line. Anyone who ran low on air could ascend immediately by climbing the line, which was connected to a surface marker buoy. The trailing boat would pick up the diver at the buoy.

Slear checked the air pressure in her tank. Then the warm water exploded with foam as she tumbled backward off the boat. Her dive computer, fastened along with a compass to a hose on her air tank, started automatically. This dive, on March 19, 1997, would be her 61st, a proud achievement for the soft-spoken woman who spent most of her working life near Philadelphia sitting at a computer.

Slear followed the exhaust bubbles from divers Carrie and Gene Ferri, who were kicking leisurely over the reef at a depth of 75 feet. About 20 minutes into the dive, the current picked up, forcing Slear to search out a handhold. She tried to slow her headlong swoop along the reef, but the invisible stream of sea water thrust the divers relentlessly north. Slear sailed downcurrent, colliding with Carrie. *Wow*, Slear thought, *this current must be at least three knots.* She clung stubbornly to a sponge, her arms strained to the aching point.

With her air supply running low, Slear indicated to Frank that she was going up. But nearing 20 feet, she felt the slack buoy line jerk taut. A crosscurrent was dragging her away from the other divers. *I'm going to pull Kevin away too,* she thought, and let go of the line.

After pausing twice to decompress, Slear inflated her buoyancy vest at a depth of ten feet and popped to the surface about 100 yards north of the marker buoy. She turned in a circle until she spotted the dive boat.

"Hey!" she yelled, waving. "Over here!" Vaughn Campbell, the boat's skipper, did not hear her. *They'll spot me in a minute,* she thought.

But now the strong current began sweeping her away from the boat. Slear pressed her mask tighter on her face and bit down hard on the rubber mouthpiece of her snorkel. *Just relax,* she kept telling herself. *The boat will pick me up soon.* But within minutes, she'd been carried north between the green

slopes of Goat Island and Little Tobago, toward the empty expanse of the Atlantic Ocean.

Gene Ferri, who had organized the trip from the United States,
hauled himself into the rocking boat and was followed shortly
by the other divers. "Wait a minute," Gene said, looking
around. "Where's Vivienne?"

"She was the first one to leave the reef," Frank replied. "I saw
her on the line, and she was doing fine." Five minutes passed,
then ten. The divers searched the entire reef area around Little Tobago, but there was no sign of Slear. Vaughn Campbell
shifted the outboard motors into gear and turned the boat in
an expanding circle.

Frank radioed the dive shop requesting that other boats
join the search. When he set down the microphone, his voice
broke. "Lord," he moaned, "in all my years of diving, I've never
had this happen."

Gene remembered that Slear had complained of a minor
decompression headache after yesterday's dive. *I hope she didn't
suffer a ruptured lung or a stroke,* he thought.

"We'll keep looking," he said, hoping his voice sounded confident. "She's got to be nearby."

Tumbling wildly through breaking ten-foot waves, Slear had
been caught in a tangle of rough current, wind-driven chop
and shifting tide, powerful forces struggling for dominance near
the offshore islands. As a wave flooded her snorkel, she spit out
warm, salty water. The midday sun beat on her head, making her
queasy. With the trade wind—which was blowing steadily from

the northeast—funneled against the fast north-running current, the sea was carrying her ever farther from the search area.

Slear fought a cold stab of panic. *I'm too low in the water for them to see me*, she thought, inflating her buoyancy vest to maximum pressure. It lifted her shoulders higher in the chop, but still the steady current carried her north.

This is crazy, she told herself. *Search parties will be here soon. Just stay afloat and keep a sharp lookout.*

By 1:40 p.m. about a dozen boats were crisscrossing the reefs and channels between Tobago and Little Tobago. Reggie Mac Lean, the general manager of the Blue Waters Inn where the dive shop is located, requested a search plane and boat from the Trinidad and Tobago Coast Guard. Officials couldn't guarantee immediate support.

Mac Lean called a private charter company. "Get a plane up here fast," he stressed. "I don't care how much it costs. We have to find this woman."

Carrie Ferri crouched in the prow of the dive boat, gazing through binoculars at the choppy swells. Ever since Slear had joined the scuba group, Carrie had been her mentor and occasional dive buddy on junkets across the Caribbean. Now Carrie felt a numbing sadness that her friend might be dead. "Hang in there, Viv," she whispered. "We'll find you."

But the dive boat began to roll violently, and green waves sloshed over the prow. Clinging to the rail for support, Gene Ferri shook his head. "That's it," he said sharply. "We can't risk losing six to try to find one." Campbell throttled back the outboards and turned to shore.

Unable to fight the clammy grip of seasickness, Slear retched painfully. *Where is the boat?* she wondered.

She looked at her dive computer. Four hours had elapsed since she'd lost sight of the boat. A brutal realization swept over her: *They'll be searching for a submerged body, not a floating survivor.* "Nobody's looking for me," she said aloud.

Overhead, hook-beaked frigate birds circled, dipping low, their reptilian eyes probing her. She kept wondering if they saw her as a potential meal of carrion. "I'm not dead yet!" she yelled. *Estimate your position,* she thought, trying to stay calm.

Slear had been watching the green spine of Tobago's Main Ridge Forest Reserve to the southwest. Now, as higher swells rolled in from the Atlantic, the ridge that had been her landmark was disappearing.

Oh, God! Where'd the land go? Tobago was now due south and lower on the horizon. The trade wind and current were carrying her around the northeastern tip of the island.

"I'm going to have to save myself," Slear said, realizing that she could no longer wait to be rescued, a helpless castaway. She began to kick powerful, rhythmic strokes with her long, blue fins. She would swim against this remorseless current until her strength was gone. *The sea will not take me,* she vowed.

The divers at the Blue Waters Inn stared silently at the search boats in Batteau Bay. Neither the private charter plane nor the Coast Guard aircraft had located Slear.

"We'll find her," the unflappable Mac Lean tried to reassure the Americans. Gene Ferri glanced at the shade line that had already covered the crescent beach. "It'll be dark in an hour, Reggie."

"We can't lose hope," Mac Lean replied.

Her legs growing heavier with each stroke of her fins, Slear forced aside any thought of resting. She pictured her boyfriend, Larry, back in Edgewater Park, New Jersey. About now, he'd be home from work, feeding her frisky black Labrador puppy, Xena, and her brown rabbit, Homer. That life seemed to exist on another planet.

She imagined her parents in central Pennsylvania receiving the phone call announcing her death. No! She would not fall into this mental ambush. There was room for only one thought: *Don't stop kicking until you reach shore.*

The sky still retained diffuse sunlight when she heard the unmistakable rumble of a boat engine. Kicking hard, Slear thrust her body high on a wave crest and caught a glimpse of a white cabin cruiser.

"I'm here!" she shouted, waving a fin above her head. The boat disappeared in the shadows.

Slear's throat swelled with anguish. *Kick,* she resolved, fighting the current that took her away from the shore. *Just keep kicking.* Suddenly she heard a hiss, and saw the milky wash of surf breaking on steep, weedy rock. *Landfall!* she thought, as a wave lifted her toward the dark boulders on Tobago's northeastern cape.

Grabbing instinctively for support, Slear flinched as razor-edged barnacles slashed her hands. Then another crashing wave smashed her against the rock, and she was dragged help-lessly down the cliff.

"No!" she shouted. Realizing she could break an arm or sever an artery, Slear kicked backward into the very sea she'd fought for the past seven hours.

Chilled and exhausted, her hands bleeding, Slear watched dully as the cliffs faded into shadows. Then she snapped into focus. "This is not going to be the end," she vowed aloud.

Glancing once more at her compass, she forced her legs to move her south, toward shore. A three-quarter moon rose, gilding the water like burnished copper. She saw a twinkling cluster of lights and thought it must be a village on Tobago's northeastern coast. She had no way to gauge the distance, but it gave her hope.

A sudden, chilling rain squall lashed the swells and pelted her with stinging drops. The squall passed, and once again she concentrated on the distant constellation of lights, kicking steadily with legs that no longer seemed attached to her body.

Slear faced seaward and saw the dazzling aura of a cruise ship angling toward the festive ports of Trinidad. She pictured people in flowery shirts sipping margaritas as steel bands lilted gay rhythms.

Carrie Ferri lay sleepless as the squall pelted the roof of the inn. She heard a heavier surf begin to rumble on the beach. Her mind jumped between images of her friend's dead body swept along the dark swells, and of Vivienne struggling alone in the rain-swept sea.

Her friend was no "iron woman" athlete; Slear had never excelled in sports, and with her current life, it was difficult to find time for exercise. But Carrie knew that Vivienne was strong inside. Without a college degree, the young woman had begun in a modest clerical position, then risen through the ranks of the federal agency that regulates credit unions. Volunteering for after-hours computer training, she achieved a professional position. *If anyone can make it,* Carrie thought, *Vivienne will.*

Slear's mind clouded with overpowering fatigue, and her eyes slipped shut. Moments passed as she dozed, only to snap awake.

The rising sun was hot when she saw creamy surf in an open bay to her left. Houses were perched in the hills above coconut trees and water—Bloody Bay on Tobago's northern coast. *Survival lay only a half-mile away!*

Slear rolled her aching body over and resumed her endless kicking. Suddenly, the sea tilted cruelly and slammed her into a whirlpool of choppy waves. She had drifted into treacherous, churning water near a reef.

"Not again," she moaned. Unless she fought her way back to sea, she'd be battered to death on half-hidden jagged coral.

Her arms and legs wracked by spasms of pain, Slear kicked weakly away from the taunting promise of the bay. Now a trade wind began to kick up chop against the current. She lay inert in the water, utterly drained.

Turning landward one more time, Slear was stunned. Before her was a perfect crescent of sand ringed with coconut trees, curving beneath a green hillside dotted with houses. It looked like a picture postcard.

Using the last of her willpower, Slear forced her legs to maintain a steady stroke through the surf until she felt the strange solidity of land against her shoulder. The surf lifted her higher onto the sloping beach where she flopped like a stranded seal.

I'm alive! The thought seemed so improbable that she almost laughed. Then she heard *real* laughter—the piping chuckle of approaching Tobagonian schoolgirls, neat in their white blouses.

Later that afternoon Slear sat with Carrie and Gene Ferri on a shady patio of the Blue Waters Inn, enjoying a soft trade wind rustling the tropical foliage. Looking at a calm sea, it was hard to believe that Vivienne had been lost for 27½ hours, fighting currents and riptides for about 14 miles.

COURTING
DISASTER

DEATHFALL AT DENALI PASS

BY PETER MICHELMORE

"What a feeling!" Michael Angove exclaimed, hugging his climbing buddy, Brian McKinley. The two men were standing on Mt. McKinley's 20,320-foot peak in Alaska. It was the evening of Thursday, May 4, 1995, and they had been climbing for nine hours straight.

"Fabulous!" McKinley rasped in the thin, clean air. Not even the wind chill of minus 10 degrees Fahrenheit could quell their triumph at climbing North America's highest peak.

The two friends snapped pictures of each other. Then Angove took the cell phone they carried and called his wife, Faith, in Spokane, Washington.

"We're standing on top of Mt. McKinley!" he announced.

"Great!" she said with obvious pleasure. "Now I want you home!"

Angove asked her to get word to McKinley's wife of three months, Pam, who was in San Diego, and then he folded up the phone. His watch showed 7 p.m. Through a break in the clouds he saw that the sun was still in the southern sky. He figured the 3,000-foot descent to their camp would take three hours. "We'll have plenty of light for the return," he said.

McKinley gestured his friend into the lead position and Angove took off, the 50-foot red nylon rope that connected their body harnesses trailing behind him. Two hours later they reached Denali Pass, a snow-covered saddle between the mountain's north and south peaks.

The climbers crossed the pass and continued down Mt. McKinley's west flank. Their slightly diagonal path put the mountainside's steep, icy slope to their right. Sharp, pointed crampons bound to their boots crunched into the wind-hardened snow. If they slipped, they could slide hundreds of feet before regaining a foothold. Angove held his three-foot-long ice ax by the shaft, ready to sink the pick into the snow if he fell.

Suddenly, from behind, Angove heard a hoarse cry: "Stop!" Whirling around, he gaped in horror. McKinley was skidding on his side down the icy incline. Before Angove could react, the rope between them tightened and he felt himself yanked over. He hit the slope on his back, his body tobogganing downhill at breakneck speed. With a mighty overarm sweep Angove slammed his ice ax into the face of the slope. Its steel pick hit the rock-hard snow and bounced off.

Soon Angove was in free fall, flying headfirst down the mountain. He shut his eyes against the cold rush of air. He felt no panic—only a shock of finality. *This is it!* he thought. *We're dead men!*

His back hit the slope with a crunch. He heard the buckles

of his pack screech over the ice. Then his head spun and everything went black.

With their shared love of the outdoors, Mike Angove, 31, a Navy lieutenant, and Brian McKinley, 37, a lieutenant commander, had hit it off from the day they met. That was six years earlier, when they were both students at the Navy's postgraduate school in Monterey, Califorinia. Wiry, dark-haired Angove, raised in Washington State, had been scaling mountains since age 18. "The thrill," he told his friend, "is getting to places that are incredibly difficult to reach." McKinley—an energetic hiker and rock-climber from Towson, Maryland—had become an eager convert to the sport.

Together they climbed Mt. Rainier and twice reached the peak of Mt. Whitney. But after graduating from the Navy school in December 1991, they'd been posted to opposite sides of the world—Angove to Guam; McKinley to Florida. This Alaska trip marked their first climb together again. When Angove first suggested a climb to the top of Mt. McKinley, his friend agreed instantly. "After all," McKinley pointed out, "the mountain *does* have my name."

Meeting in Los Angeles, they traveled to the base camp and then began the 14-day ascent. During the second week, they linked up with two others: Roderick Hancock, 26, and Deborah Robertson, 28. On May 2, the four climbers pitched camp on an undulating plateau of snow and rock 17,200 feet above sea level. Two days later they would make their final assault on Mt. McKinley's south peak, its highest point.

Hancock and Robertson were first to reach the summit.

Barely 15 minutes after starting their descent, they met Angove and McKinley on their way up. "We made it!" Robertson
called out. "See you guys back at camp."

Slowly Angove's senses cleared. *I'm alive!* he realized with a
shock. *I survived!*

He felt his body sway gently to and fro and saw that he was
hanging horizontally, face up in his rope harness in a narrow
crevasse. Below him the pale blue ice disappeared into a black
void.

Twenty-five feet or so straight up, he saw daylight. On the
rim of the crevasse he saw one of his mittens, and he became
aware that his right hand was bare and stiffening with cold. His
ice ax, he realized, was gone.

The rope ran up the middle of the crevasse and disappeared
over the ridge above him. *I'm still attached to Brian,* Angove
thought. His friend must be lodged against something.

Hauling on the rope, Angove righted his body. "Brian!
Are you okay?" he shouted. He cocked an ear. Nothing. *Unconscious,* Angove thought. *But in what condition?*

Angove figured he could work his way up the rope, hand
over hand. Then he stopped himself. *If Brian is wedged behind
a loose rock, I could dislodge him.* Gripping openings in the ice
wall, he began hauling himself up—first a handhold, then a
foothold, inch by inch.

At his fourth step, the crampon fell from his left boot, van-
ishing in the void below. The fingers of his bare hand were
turning chalk-white, the beginning of frostbite. Angove kicked
a boot into a crack in the ice and climbed on.

Twenty minutes later he finally hauled himself over the lip of the ravine. Snatching up his mitten, he pulled it onto his right hand, then pushed the hand under his coat and held it tightly against his stomach for warmth.

Ahead of him, the rope snaked off until it disappeared over a ridge of snow. Moving gingerly over the ice, Angove followed it. A few feet over the ridge, McKinley lay in a fetal position against a pinnacle of ice. "Brian," Angove called, "let me help you up!"

Kneeling at McKinley's side, Angove raised him to a half-sitting position. With the movement an eerie, wheezing sound came from McKinley's throat. Never in his life had Angove seen a man die. Yet he knew that he'd just heard his friend's last breath. He reached for McKinley's wrist. There was no pulse.

A sob exploded from Angove's throat. He felt a rush of guilt and loneliness. "Brian!" he murmured, holding his friend close. "I'm so sorry!" *All our mountain climbing,* Angove thought, *the trip here—it was all my idea!* Suddenly he felt a presence in the air around him—as if his friend's spirit were leaving his body. It seemed so real that Angove had an urge to reach out and try to touch it.

His own shivering brought him back to the present. The sun was gone; it was fiercely cold. *Snap out of it!* he told himself. *You'll have to go on alone.*

Looking around, Angove saw a high knob of snow about half a mile away down the mountain. He knew their base camp was located just below it.

Suddenly he remembered the cell phone. It was programmed

with the number of the park ranger station in Talkeetna, 50 miles southeast. But when he punched the buttons, "No Service" flashed on the screen. The mountain, Angove realized, must be blocking the transmission.

Should he try for camp? Without an ice ax and his left crampon, Angove feared he'd never make it down the icy slope. *Stay the night here and hope for rescue in the morning? No good*, he told himself. *In this cold, if I don't keep moving, I'll die.*

Toward midnight Rod Hancock looked into the rust-colored tent where Angove and McKinley had their gear. Empty.

"They still haven't returned," he reported back to Deb Robertson, who was resting in their nearby tent. "They must've fallen—there's no other explanation."

Then he headed off through the northern twilight to a small rise on the snow field. Aiming his flashlight beam toward Denali Pass, he yelled, "Mike! . . . Brian!" No answer came back.

"No sign of them," he told Robertson. "If they're badly injured, they probably won't last the night. They'll freeze to death."

Robertson knew her friend was right. The Oregon-raised Hancock had been mountaineering for years. The two had met five years before as university students in Seattle. Robertson shared Hancock's love of adventure. They had scaled mountains across the United States and even South America.

Now as Hancock looked at his friend in the gloom of their tent, they faced a hard decision. On the climb down Robertson had been nauseated. She was too weak to join him in a search for the two missing men. Yet to go alone, unroped and in the dark, would put his own life in danger. And he couldn't risk leaving Robertson alone in her weakened condition. Right now, there could be two dead. They didn't want to risk making it four. "We'll search in the morning, Deb," he said. "You get some rest."

As Angove stared around him, he spotted a dark object up the slope against the snow. It looked like McKinley's ice ax. Untying the rope from his harness, Angove kicked his toes into the slope and, hand over hand, began pulling himself upward. Finally, exhausted, he reached the black-shafted ax and pulled it from the snow.

After a short rest he plunged the ax spike into the slope and began painfully working his way down the slippery face of the mountain. With each step he had to tug the ax free and replant it securely. He was parched with thirst, but his water was gone. The half-mile trek stretched into an infinity of time.

Angove shut everything from his thoughts. *Step . . . step . . . plant!* It became a chant in his mind.

About two hours later, rounding a bluff, still supporting his weight with the ax, Angove spotted the campsite. Slowly he maneuvered his way down. It was 2 a.m. when he reached the dome tent he had shared with McKinley. Staggering in, totally spent, he collapsed.

I have to tell someone about Brian! he thought dizzily. *I'll rest first . . . just a few minutes.*

Mike Angove sat up with a start. It was daylight. He felt a throbbing pain around his rib cage and a raging thirst. Crossing the snow to his neighbors' tent, he called out, "Rod! Deb!"

Deb Robertson yanked the tent zipper open. "We fell," said Angove, a catch in his throat. "Brian's dead."

Gently Hancock took his arm and guided him into the tent. To Robertson, Angove looked drained, almost shrunken. "Lie down, Mike," she said. "We'll take care of everything."

At her words Angove began sobbing. Tears streamed down his face as she helped him to the sleeping pad. She dropped two codeine pills into his hand and gave him a bottle of water. Then she took the cell phone and eventually got through to park ranger J. D. Swed in Talkeetna.

"There's a storm coming in this afternoon," Swed warned. "You're too exposed up there."

"We'll try to get Mike to the 14,300-foot camp," Robertson said. "I'll call again at noon."

By the time she reported back, Mike Angove was wobbly, in severe pain and unable to move. "We're staying up here with him," she said.

"We'll try to get a helicopter in there to take him off," Swed told her, "but you can't count on it. You're in for very high winds."

Swed, a trained paramedic, was worried. From what Robertson described, he suspected Angove had cerebral edema, or swelling of the brain, a symptom of high-altitude sickness. Unless Angove got out of the mountain's oxygen-thin altitude, he could lapse into a coma and die.

"If they're socked in for long," Swed told a deputy, "that man is probably not going to make it."

By early evening the wind had shifted to the north, sweeping over the ridge in a fierce Arctic blast. An attempted helicopter landing had failed, and now a blizzard of stinging snow swirled through the air. Over the gas stove in their tent, Robertson prepared a meal of freeze-dried turkey. When Hancock took it to Angove's tent, the injured man barely touched the food.

The next morning, rising wearily, Hancock looked outside. The wind-swept plateau was shrouded in thick clouds. Again he made his way to Angove's tent. Inside he extended a thermos of water. Lifting his head from his sleeping bag, Angove took only a few sips.

"Listen to me, Mike!" Hancock said sternly. "You're not going to make it through without water!"

Hoisting himself on an elbow, Angove nodded groggily and drank.

The cloud cover was too heavy for a rescue attempt that day. At night the winds pounded again. All through Sunday and Monday, as Angove grew steadily weaker, Hancock struggled to rebuild the snow wall that shielded the tents from the blasting air. Now incoherent, Angove wouldn't eat, and he drank water only because Hancock insisted. *How much longer can he last?* Hancock wondered.

Early Tuesday—nearly five days after Angove's fall—the giant wind gusts finally tapered off. Listening in their tent at 6:30, the climbers heard a distant drone. "A plane!" cried Robertson.

It was a Cessna, flying in ahead of the rescue helicopter to report wind conditions. Soon the three climbers saw a gray helicopter wheel over the ridge. At the controls pilot Doug Drury made two passes close to the tents. Wind shook the sides of the aircraft. *It's now or never!* Drury thought, easing the craft down on a protected ridge 150 yards away. "This is where we stay," he said into the intercom. "They'll have to come to us."

J. D. Swed was already sliding out of the chopper. His eyes locked on the three figures staggering toward him. Robertson and Hancock were holding Angove between them. Halfway there, Robertson stopped, exhausted. Swed ran out to meet them. As they reached the chopper, Swed helped swing Angove into the back, then hopped in after him.

"Do you want us to come back for you?" Swed yelled over the roar of the rotor.

"No!" Hancock shouted. "We'll get off by ourselves."

Slamming the door, Swed gave a thumbs-up signal to Drury. Instantly the big machine lifted and raced down the mountain.

Hancock turned to Robertson. "Let's pack up and move out, Deb," he said. "Our job's finished here."

At the Elmendorf Air Force Base hospital in Anchorage, doctors treated Angove for cerebral edema, fluid on the brain. "A few more hours," Swed said, "and he could've died."

After his release from the hospital, Michael and Faith Angove visited his parents in Spokane, Washington. On May 18 rangers recovered Brian McKinley's body. His widow, Pam, brought it to Towson, Maryland, for the funeral. Michael Angove attended.

All three survivors retain their passion for climbing. "This power to direct yourself through hardship and danger enabled Mike to survive his fall," explains Rod Hancock. "It also enabled Deb and me to help him through this ordeal. Climbing is a physical and mental endeavor like no other."

INTO THE WILD

BY KENNETH MILLER

In the high desert of southwest Utah lives a band of feral horses known as the Sulphur Herd. These small, tough animals have galloped the dusty hills since the late 1500s, when their ancestors strayed from the encampments of the conquistadores. Isolated for five centuries by the 9,000-foot peaks of the Needle Range, they are nearly identical to their Spanish forebears.

For mustang lovers, a visit to the herd's habitat is an almost mystical journey—a voyage to a time when the West was truly wild. On a Saturday in January, Tom and Tamitha Garner were making that pilgrimage in their Dodge Dakota. The couple turned off Highway 56 near Modena and headed north up a dirt road into Hamblin Valley. Soon they'd entered a stark terrain of sagebrush and red earth. A dusting of snow lay on the road, deepening gradually as the truck climbed toward the mountains.

For about 20 miles, the going was easy. Then the pickup crested a hill, cruised down the other side, and became trapped in a bumper-deep patch of white. Tom, who'd brought along a shovel, could have dug out the truck and driven back to town. But he figured this was a lone drift. Besides, the trip was his wife's 39th birthday present. He wasn't about to let her down. He cleared a path, gunned the truck over the next rise—and there, in a grove of aspens, stood the horses.

Entranced, the Garners stopped and began snapping photos. When the mustangs trotted off, the couple got back in the pickup and followed. Before long, they were getting stuck every few yards; the digging grew increasingly difficult. Returning the way they came was no longer an option: The road was too narrow and snowy to turn around in, the hills too slippery to navigate in reverse. It was 4 p.m., and darkness was approaching. "I guess we'll be spending the night," Tom said. "I'll get you home tomorrow if I have to shovel the whole road."

"You better," Tamitha laughed.

Neither knew something else was on its way: a brutal wave of blizzards.

Some people wander into disaster's path at random; others, like the Garners, are led by overpowering desire. In most respects, the two were models of practicality. Tom, 41, was a printing press operator; Tamitha was a nurse's assistant at a home for the elderly. They shared a modest home in Kearns, a Salt Lake City suburb, with their 19-year-old daughter, Krystal. The only hints of their unruly passions were their pets and their photographs.

The Garners had two dogs, two rabbits, four cats, and several terrariums full of tarantulas. Their computer's hard drive was crammed with snapshots of wild beasts—winged, clawed, and hoofed. Tom and Tamitha were as crazy about animals as they were sane about almost everything else.

Their favorite subject was wild horses. Tom was drawn to their beauty; for Tamitha, they represented freedom. Several times a year, the couple would load their cameras into the pickup and head for mustang country.

For this trip, they'd driven 400 miles to central Nevada and spent Friday—Tamitha's birthday—shooting horses they'd visited on previous outings. The highlight was to come on the way home, when they would meet the Sulphur Herd for the first time. They'd left their daughter with a rough idea of their itinerary, but the plan had been to stay for a few hours and be back in Kearns around midnight. Now they'd need to bed down in the truck instead.

They tried to call Krystal on their cell phones. No signal. Rummaging through the pickup's cab, they took inventory of their supplies. To eat: two dozen granola bars, a jar of peanut butter, and a jar of jam. To drink: 36 small bottles of water. They also had two afghans, two reflective emergency blankets, and a bag of dog food for Medusa, their basenji mix. A suitcase held jeans, sweatshirts, and tees. Tamitha had an insulated denim coat, but Tom's jacket was unlined. Their only shoes were the sneakers on their feet. If they could get out in the morning, they'd be fine. But the wind was already beginning to blow harder.

Night fell. Tom and Tamitha ate a granola bar apiece, snuggled under the blankets with Medusa, and tried to sleep. They ran the heater periodically, but it didn't do much good. The temperature outside was dropping; soon it reached five below zero.

By 2 a.m., 50-mile-an-hour gusts were buffeting the pickup, and the windows were blanketed with snow. Tamitha, who had diabetes and ulcers, began to tremble. Tom held her, and they dozed off. When they awoke around five, the storm had entered a lull and Tamitha had recovered some fight. "Either you dig out this truck or I'm going to," she said. It was still dark, but Tom put on some extra layers and gave it a try.

While he was digging, Tamitha said a prayer. On a pad of paper, she scribbled a simple will, followed by a goodbye letter to Krystal. "I'm so proud of you," she wrote, "even if we argued sometimes. Tell Grandma and Grandpa and my brothers I love them." She hid the documents in the glove compartment.

After an hour of shoveling, Tom started the engine. The truck lurched forward ten yards, then foundered. And despite the garbage bags he'd wrapped around his socks to keep them dry, his feet were soaked.

"Too much snow," he said. "I'm so sorry I got you into this."

Tamitha hugged him. "We got into it together. We'll get out together too."

Back in Kearns, Krystal was frantic. Usually, Tamitha phoned or sent text messages several times a day. Now Krystal's calls were going straight to voice mail. "Mom," she said, "where are you? Are you hurt?"

By Sunday evening, Krystal had alerted other family members. Her grandparents and an uncle, Tamitha's brother Jack Retallick, set up a command post in the Garners' living room. All they knew was that Tom and Tamitha were somewhere near the border of southern Utah and Nevada.

Krystal contacted the Salt Lake County sheriff's department, which alerted authorities in the Garners' last known locations. The relatives began calling hospitals, ranger stations, the highway patrol. No one could offer any information. And no one was willing to mount a search-and-rescue operation for a couple who seemed to have taken an extra day of vacation.

In Hamblin Valley, the blizzard worsened, the wind piling drifts around the pickup. Tom, who'd been an Eagle Scout, knew it was best to stay put and wait for rescuers. Besides, getting wet was the greatest danger—a shortcut to hypothermia. He and Tamitha spent Monday huddled under the blankets, smoking cigarettes and listening to the radio—talk shows and weather reports, all bemoaning the storm.

Tamitha grew weaker by the hour, occasionally vomiting blood. After Tom found her will, she persuaded him to write his own. That night, when he ate a granola bar, she left hers untouched. Once he was snoring, she stashed it under the seat. Tom might need it later, but she surely wasn't going to live until morning.

To her surprise, she woke on Tuesday feeling stronger. The blizzard was petering out, and a crowd of mustangs peered at the truck through the trees. "Look, Tom," Tamitha whispered. "Our guardian angels."

The Garners didn't know it, but searchers were now trying to track them down. Jack had found a file marked "Mustangs" on the couple's computer, with downloads showing locations of various herds. He'd passed along that data to the authorities. Hundreds of volunteers—along with members of several county sheriff's departments and the Utah and Nevada Civil Air Patrol—were combing 5,000 square miles of frigid wilderness.

Although the wind was still howling, the couple could hear airplanes flying somewhere over the cloud cover—one every 50 minutes or so. Tom, remembering a scouting survival tip, cut the vanity mirror off the truck's visor. When he heard an engine, he leaned out the window and flashed a signal. After sunset, he used the headlights, flickering them in sets of three.

The rescue efforts were so widely scattered, though, that few searchers came near the Garners. Most of the passing aircraft were commercial jets. Even when a search plane circled half a mile away, it was easy to miss a gray truck buried in snow.

That night, while her husband slept, Tamitha tried a handful of dog food. Tom would never eat it, she thought, and it wasn't that bad. She'd leave the rest of the granola bars for him.

As the days passed, and the cycle of storm and clearing continued, the Garners realized that their best hope of survival was to abandon the truck and walk back the way they'd come. But they knew they couldn't hike 20 miles wearing only sneakers. "We might make it," Tom told his wife, "but we'd lose our feet to frostbite and spend the rest of our lives in wheelchairs." He'd seen a Discovery Channel documentary in which a couple in similar straits had made snowshoes out of their car seats.

They spent Saturday getting ready and planned to leave the next day. To make one pair of snowshoes, Tom cut two squares of foam out of the backseats. He and Tamitha crammed necessities into their suitcase and a garbage bag. Along with dry clothing, blankets, and the remaining food, they packed a tool kit, three umbrellas, and their camera equipment—they couldn't bear to leave it behind.

On Sunday, it snowed. Tamitha groaned at the delay, but the couple spent the day communicating in a way they hadn't since their courtship. They talked about favorite movies and music. They made plans to renovate their house. Tamitha wanted a purple bedroom; Tom wasn't so sure.

Their cell phone alarms rang at six the next morning. Tom cut up the front seats for the second pair of snowshoes and fastened both sets to their feet with bungee cords. Snowdrifts blocked the truck doors, so he heaved the suitcase and garbage bag out the window. Medusa jumped out, and the Garners squeezed out after her.

The snow in the roadway ranged from knee- to hip-deep, but Tom's improvised footwear kept him from sinking more than a few inches, even with the weight of the suitcase he carried. Tamitha, dragging the garbage bag, wasn't so lucky. The snowshoes fit poorly on her smaller feet; they kept coming loose, and after an hour or so, she tore them off in exasperation. Tom strapped them to his back for later use.

"I'll make you a trail," he said. He walked sideways, tamping down the snow by putting his left foot where his right had been, then using the suitcase to flatten the space between.

The technique worked, but it slowed their progress even more. By late afternoon, their energy was spent. They'd made it only a couple of miles.

They set up camp in a pine grove, laying their blankets beneath the canopy of branches. After gathering a pile of twigs, they sprayed it with flammable deodorant and ignited it with a cigarette lighter. They propped their sneakers near the flames to dry. Then, sheltered by their umbrellas and using the snowshoes as cushions, they sat by the fire until they stopped shivering.

When Tamitha took off her gloves, Tom saw that the fingers of her right hand looked blue—a sign of frostbite. Again he told her how sorry he was. "Don't be," she said. "If we come out of this alive, what's a few fingers? I'll just learn to brush my teeth differently."

They spent most of the night at the fire. Before dawn, the sky cleared and a shooting star streaked overhead. "See that?" Tom said. "I think we're going to make it."

By the second Tuesday after Tom and Tamitha's disappearance, authorities had given them up for dead. Investigators, suspecting foul play, were checking pawnshops along the Nevada border for the couple's possessions. Searchers were looking for corpses.

Meanwhile, the Garners—hungry and exhausted—kept walking. The day was sunny, in the 40s, and the slushy snow made every step a chore. After a few miles, Tom wanted nothing more than to lie down. Tamitha saw him wavering. "Come on," she shouted. "Krystal's waiting! Can't you hear her? She's yelling, 'Daddy, I need you!'"

To lighten their loads, they transferred a few essentials to the garbage bag. Before long, however, they were both too tired to continue. As they made camp, they heard coyotes howling. They hoped their fire would keep predators away.

On the road Wednesday morning, the snow began to thin,

which meant Tom could abandon his clumsy snowshoes. Tamitha, though, began to hallucinate. She heard laughter, smelled sizzling steak and baking cookies.

And she found herself growing angry. She quarreled with Tom about which way to turn at a fork in the path; they clashed again when she spotted a No Trespassing sign on a fence post and wanted to see if there was a house beyond it. He won both arguments, and she stormed off ahead of him.

Tamitha was alone when she heard the sound of an engine. "That damn wind," she muttered. Then she rounded the bend and saw a beautiful sight: a road grader, laboring uphill with its snowplow lowered. She ran toward it, waving the emergency blanket and yelling, "Thank you!"

As Tom and Medusa straggled up, the driver asked, "Are you the couple everyone's been looking for?"

"Yes!" Tamitha shouted, wrapping him in a bone-crushing hug.

Even when everyone else around her was losing hope, Krystal had stayed optimistic. "I knew how bullheaded my mom and dad were," she recalls. "I figured they'd come back home. I just didn't know when."

She drove 300 miles with her uncle Jack to a hospital in Cedar City, where the extended family gathered at her parents' bedside. That evening, Tom and Tamitha ate a hearty dinner, their first in 12 days. They were diagnosed with dehydration as well as frostbitten hands and feet. To the doctors' amazement, they were otherwise unharmed and unlikely to suffer any permanent damage.

The couple were discharged from the hospital the next morning. They didn't go straight home, however. First they attended the funeral of a stranger: Leroy Davenport, 37, a local volunteer who'd spent the previous Saturday searching for them. He'd gone to bed feeling ill and died in his sleep of an undiagnosed heart condition. The Garners embraced Davenport's widow and offered tearful thanks.

Within two weeks, Tom and Tamitha were back at their jobs. But their sojourn in the snow had changed them. In the future, they would travel more carefully and cherish each other—and their daughter—more deeply. In fact, they planned to revisit the site of their ordeal after the spring thaw, to see the wild horses once again and renew their wedding vows.

"Our bond is stronger than ever," Tamitha says. "We've been to hell and back and lived to tell."

LOST

BY LYNN ROSELLINI

At eight months shy of 50, Charlie Hench had the happy-go-lucky air of an unfettered younger man. A former Michigan State rugby player, he was six feet tall and could bench-press 315 pounds. In recent years, he'd run with the bulls in Spain, canoed through the Boundary Waters of Minnesota, and hiked the Sierra backcountry in California with a group of friends.

These days, though, Hench wasn't feeling so great. His right knee was hurting from a ligament he'd torn 30 years earlier. His father had recently died. And he and his girlfriend of seven years, Julie McGuigan, were going through another rocky patch. Their relationship was a tumultuous one, Hench admits. She had, he says, "this incredible need I didn't know how to satisfy."

So Hench did what he'd often do when things got tense: He cooked up an adventure to get lost in. This time a solo hike across the Sierra Nevada sounded especially appealing. "I'm getting soft," Hench told McGuigan. "If I don't do it now, I never will."

Hench is not the first person one would think of to undertake a five-day hike across an imposing mountain range. He often joked that for his group camping trips, he'd sooner pack a case of beer than a sleeping bag. In addition to being a cutup, he was a klutz at work, stumbling on things at job sites as an engineer with the California Department of Transportation in Cambria, on the central coast of California. He was fun but reckless, steering a car with his knees while pounding the dash in time to U2's "New Year's Day." Once, he accidentally rolled a company truck over an embankment, somehow emerging unscathed. On numerous occasions, "you'd think, This is it—we're taking him to the hospital for sure," says his longtime friend John Luchetta. "Then he'd get up and dust himself off."

Many in Hench's tight-knit group of friends found his wild streak endearing; all of them admired him for his generosity. Want someone to bust up your patio with a jackhammer? Need help roofing your house? Call Charlie. "He even made a bench in honor of my grandmother when she died," says close friend Steve Baliban.

Hench had plenty of help, then, in preparing for his solo Sierra quest. His friends supplied rain gear, freeze-dried meals, and a headlamp; one called up Google Earth on his computer to plot Hench's mountain route. If Luchetta and the group had misgivings about the trip, they didn't say so, figuring that if Hench had gotten this far, he could survive anything.

His gear neatly stuffed in a nylon backpack, Hench hitched a ride to the Sierra foothills. On a Monday evening, he made camp at the edge of Lake Edison, 9,200 feet up the western slope of the range. He'd brought five days' worth of food, a portable stove, a sleeping bag, a tent, and a fishing rod. He sat on a log, tending a campfire and gazing at a canopy of stars. He was happy to be there. Life seemed easier in the clear mountain air. He took out a pen and wrote, "Into the Wild. Ramblings of Charlie on a solo trans-Sierra Nevada, Sept. 17–22."

The next morning, a campground employee gave Hench a ride to the trailhead to start his 15-mile hike to Lake Italy. As the truck pulled away, the driver mentioned that a storm was expected to blow through later in the week. "Don't know whether it's going to snow," he told Hench.

For the first ten miles of the trip, the trail was well maintained, with a clear dirt path and markers on the trees. But it petered out above the tree line, and Hench got lost several times, in part because his new compass wasn't working. Late on Wednesday, he pitched his tent on the stark shore of the lake. "Holy moly, I made it," he wrote.

As he lay in his sleeping bag that night, he heard the wind pick up until it was ripping across the lake with 50-mph gusts. By Thursday morning, the snow was coming down sideways.

Early-season storms in the Sierra Nevada are rare, surprising tourists who venture into the backcountry in T-shirts, lulled by Indian summer temperatures down below. On a single day a few years back, more than two dozen hikers were stranded at different points in the mountains when an October storm roared across the range, dropping four feet of snow. Three experienced climbers, blue and frostbitten, were fortunate to have been rescued from the face of El Capitan in Yosemite National Park, 60 miles northwest of Hench's campsite; two others in their party perished.

"Not sure what to do so am hunkering down for a spell," Hench wrote on Thursday after whiteout conditions drove two-foot drifts against his tent. Hikers elsewhere in the range that day reported that the wind was "from another planet," snapping trees with trunks eight feet in diameter. Hench, meanwhile, added a note in his diary: "May hang out here for a day."

Julie McGuigan was at her desk when a coworker stopped by to inquire about Hench. "Did you know there's a storm coming in?" he asked. McGuigan, a 46-year-old biologist, loved Hench's high spirits. He was the kind of guy who would do a funny little dance in the middle of her living-room floor just for fun. Who else would present her with a Valentine's Day gift of a backyard bat house? She glanced out the office window. Sierra storms often translate locally into clouds and rain; the sky outside was ominously dark. "He'll be okay," she said, reasoning that Hench always found a way.

When Hench woke up on Friday morning, the sun was out and clouds drifted lazily across the blue sky. He broke camp and began climbing toward Italy Pass, 1,200 feet above the lake. He planned to follow the pass across the Sierra Nevada ridgeline, then drop down to the eastern slope. But now, with the trail buried, Hench was forced to hop from one slippery boulder to the next, over treacherous gullies of deep snow.

Near noon, he reached a ridge. Doesn't look right, he thought. Though he didn't realize it at the time, Hench had made a wrong turn and ended up on a precipitous saddle north of the pass. He was trying to figure out his location when he fell, finding himself sprawled on a boulder, his wrist throbbing and blood trickling down the right side of his face. He looked out blankly at a lake sparkling several hundred feet below.

"Solo trans-Sierra hike!" he said out loud. "You idiot!"

His walking stick, map, and glasses were gone. His right wrist was on fire, broken for sure. Rising slowly to his feet, Hench straightened his backpack, his two-piece fishing pole still attached, but slipped again, scraping an elbow. He tried to steady himself and fell once more, this time skidding down the rock-strewn face and landing on his back on a granite ledge about the size of a grand piano. A sheer cliff dropped all the way to the valley floor, several hundred feet below. There was no going up or down. He was trapped.

Hench's fishing buddy Grant Krueger was a worrier. When Hench didn't show up at the trailhead where they'd planned to meet on day five, he called McGuigan. Soon the cell phones of Hench's friends were buzzing.

Within hours they had a plan. One team would trace Hench's intended route from Lake Edison up the western side of the range. Krueger and another buddy would start at the trailhead near Bishop and track Hench's route backward, up the eastern slope. The teams would meet at the summit. They'd alerted the Fresno and Inyo County police departments, which would each send out a search-and-rescue team on foot and by air first thing Monday morning, 48 hours after Hench failed to show at the trailhead. At home near San Luis Obispo, McGuigan would run the central command, feeding identifying information about Hench to county rescue teams and logging names and contact numbers on a big board.

In Bishop on Monday, Krueger had one last thought before embarking. A former colleague, David Grah, knew the Sierra backcountry well from hiking its peaks and piloting his small plane over the range. Krueger left a note at Grah's office in town, asking for help in the search for Hench.

"Saturday, Sept. 22. Yesterday was the worst day of my life, save the day I watched my dad die," Hench wrote. Wet, freezing, and exhausted, he had found just enough room on the ledge to set up his tent. Inside, he surveyed the situation: no signal mirror, a broken compass, no cell phone reception. At least he had a few days' worth of food: freeze-dried beef stew, granola bars, trail mix, and a package of pancake mix. Search teams would come for him soon. Until then, he would stay calm. "I was a fool to try this alone," he wrote. "I hope to make it out."

But another 48 hours dragged by, and the only things he felt were pain and fear. His throbbing wrist was swollen to twice its size, and he had a huge scrape near his eye. Though the sky was clear, by early Monday the bitter cold had sunk deep into his bones.

He heard helicopters thumping across Lake Italy that afternoon, and his spirits lifted. It was just a matter of time before he'd see his friends and McGuigan again, he thought as tears rolled down his cheeks. Tying a red stuff sack onto the tip of his fishing pole, he gamely waved the makeshift flag. The sound of the choppers faded.

That night, he wrote in his diary, "I want the nightmare to end." When he pulled aside his tent flap and looked outside, the stars that had seemed so comforting back at Lake Edison were now cold and far away. "I brought along a cheap compass," he wrote, "and I'm paying for it with my life."

By dusk on Tuesday, a handful of Caltrans engineers had arrived at different campsites just below Italy Pass. The mood was grim as Grant Krueger and a friend from Bishop set up their cooking kit on the eastern slope. Choppers had circled overhead all day, sometimes just 100 feet aboveground, with no sign of Hench. "Someone should have found him by now," Krueger told McGuigan on the satellite phone he'd taken with him.

She was racked with worry, but, keeping it to herself, said, simply, "No news here. Get some sleep."

Earlier that day—Hench's fifth on the ledge—he again heard helicopters, then . . . nothing. He had lost his most detailed map but had another, which he pored over, trying to discover where he'd made his mistake. Suddenly it was obvious: His wrong turn had taken him at least a half mile from Italy Pass, so the rescue teams were searching a distant area. "I thought they'd given up looking for me," he says.

Determined to make it off the ledge, Hench packed his gear and attempted to crawl over the loose rocks, using his good hand to steady and his right elbow to pull. He needed to get closer to Italy Pass. But after 40 feet, he got stuck. As darkness closed in, he sat on a rock and pulled his sleeping bag around him.

On a piece of cardboard, he began writing a will. He would leave Krueger his fishing boat. McGuigan and his five brothers would split the house in Cambria. A full moon rose over the granite peaks. He was going to die, just like this: a big fool, stranded on a cliff in the Sierra Nevada.

At his home 50 miles away in Bishop, Dave Grah noticed the full moon shining outside his window. He hadn't slept well all week, thinking about Hench and the note Grant Krueger had left on his desk. Thirty years earlier, his brother had nearly died in a fall off an icy Sierra cliff while hiking alone. The accident occurred at an altitude of 12,000 feet, on a saddle between peaks northwest of Italy Pass. Grah couldn't shake the feeling that maybe Hench was in the same spot.

At 6:30 the next morning—the start of a clear, cool day—he powered up his 1950 Cessna 170 and climbed up the range's eastern flank and over Italy Pass. Most pilots allow at least a thousand feet of clearance when crossing the Sierra to avoid sudden updrafts and downdrafts; wrecked planes can be found here and there across the range. But Grah knew there was no way he could spot Hench from well above the peaks. He would be cautious but fly low, scouring every square mile of the granite wilderness.

He soared past the saddle, straining to see anything that would suggest a human form among the rocks. Nothing. Grah felt deflated. It was probably silly to have come, he thought. He banked the Cessna around Lake Edison, then skirted the cliffs once more.

Suddenly, level with the passenger window and about a football field away, Grah spotted a man standing on a snow-covered ledge—in almost the exact same place where his brother had fallen. The man was waving a stick with a bit of red fabric on the end.

Hench saw the silver Cessna dip its wings. It was so close, it looked like it was flying straight into the mountain. He shouted. He danced. A few minutes later, the plane reappeared, this time trailed by a California Highway Patrol helicopter. The chopper crew dropped a message on a line attached to a weight. "If you're Charlie Hench," read the message, "raise one arm. If you're hurt, raise the other." Hench raised both arms.

The mountainside was almost vertical, and shifting wind currents made it difficult for the chopper to hover in place. But pilot Bill Dixon managed to ease the aircraft into a horizontal gap in the rock and to rest one set of skids on the narrow ledge. Flight officer Andrea Brown leaned out and motioned for Hench to step forward. He shook his head no. "I could tell he was scared to death," Brown says. "It was slippery, and if he fell, it was hundreds of feet down."

Dixon maneuvered the chopper a few feet closer. "You need to come now," Brown mouthed to Hench. He lifted his wrist to indicate it was fractured; as he stepped on the skid, Brown grabbed him by the belt, pulling him inside. The Fresno County Sheriff's Department would later report that on a scale of difficulty ranging from 1 to 10, the rescue of Charlie Hench was a 9.9.

In San Luis Obispo Wednesday morning, an announcement came over the Caltrans PA system: "They found Charlie Hench." Cheers erupted throughout the building.

Grant Krueger, who was at that moment on a trail on the eastern side of the ridge just below the summit, received the news on his satellite phone.

Back in Bishop, Grah called McGuigan and scratched his head, trying to make sense of the coincidence of two men falling off a mountaintop in exactly the same spot.

Hench phoned his girlfriend from a hospital in Bishop, where doctors had inserted 12 pins in his right wrist and treated him for chipped vertebrae and abrasions. McGuigan cried when she heard Hench's voice. "He broke down crying too," she says. "He told me he'd sat all night on a rock, thinking it was over for him."

Hench now bears a two-inch scar next to his right eye, and he will always have the pins in his wrist. He and McGuigan are planning to move in together. Occasionally, while walking a construction site or mowing his back lawn, he flashes back to his time on the icy ledge and a current shoots through his body. He remembers the friends who kept up their search for him. Maybe, he now thinks, a man doesn't find himself by running with the bulls or hiking solo across the mountains. Maybe getting lost in the clouds isn't the only way to dream. Maybe a man can find himself warm at home, surrounded by the people who love him.

JOURNEY TO THE SOUTH POLE

TODD PITOCK

One eye was frozen shut. He hadn't slept in days, and he was hallucinating.

The visions had been appearing for thirty-six hours already. Out of one eye, he could see his grandfather's house, but when he turned to look, it would disappear. His grandfather, wife, sisters, and nephew would all appear behind him. He knew they weren't really there—his grandfather had died in 2002, and the others were back in the United States—but he figured he'd go with it anyway.

"We're going to be okay," he told his visions. "We're going to make it."

He kept repeating the last line, knowing even as he spoke that his chances of survival were diminishing by the hour.

Todd Carmichael, a 45-year-old adventurer from Philadelphia, had spent thirty-nine days alone in Antarctica, where he'd walked almost 700 miles pulling a sled he'd named Betty the

Pig. He'd lost fifty pounds, and his chest was as tight as if his ribs were bound in plaster. The wind, sometimes reaching 100 mph, struck his body like a boxer's blows.

The Pig—piled with 260 pounds of supplies, mostly food, when Carmichael started out more than a month earlier—was down to sixty pounds. But he'd lost so much strength that the sled felt just as heavy as before. He suspected his feet were frostbitten but couldn't take off a boot to check; if he did, his foot would swell and he wouldn't be able to get the boot back on. Many trekkers had died because of bad feet.

He'd been hiking for more than forty hours without stopping. The finish line—the American-operated research station at the South Pole—was so close, he thought he could see it. The trouble was, he couldn't be sure it wasn't another hallucination.

He faced a crucial choice: Keep pulling the sled and risk imminent collapse and death. Or drop the Pig and walk on without his gear and supplies. There was no margin for error if he misjudged the distance or if the station wasn't really there.

He dropped the Pig.

"I'll come back for you," he said. "I won't leave you here. I'll come back."

Carmichael had set out on a similar journey the year before. But weeks of unrelenting blizzards—fierce weather even by Antarctica's forbidding standard—had forced him to call for rescue. Quitting had been humiliating. At home, he'd fallen into a depression.

"Failure stays with you," says Carmichael, six feet three with a shaved dome, deep-set eyes, and broad shoulders. "That feeling, from the moment I was evacuated, did not go away, day in and day out. I lived in it. I couldn't move on." The only thing that would assuage him was to try again. This time, he set his sights on a world record.

Fewer than a dozen people had ever done what Carmichael was attempting: 690 miles alone, unassisted, and unsupported—no food drops, no medical care, no animals pulling the sled—from the west coast of the Southern Ocean to the Geographic South Pole. The record for the fastest solo trek, which Carmichael was aiming to break, was held by a British woman, Hannah McKeand: 39 days, 9 hours, and 33 minutes. Carmichael would be the first American.

"It's no different from challenges other people might want to face," Carmichael said before he departed, on November 12, 2008. "This just happens to be mine. It's a very primal thing, the desire and willingness to trek across vast distances. We've loaded up carts and pulled since the dawn of man."

His wife, Lauren Hart, 42, understood this about him. They met in 2004, when she was interviewing him for a Philadelphia TV station. She asked why he'd never married. "Because I'm a trekker," he said. She recognized that his journeys weren't just a hobby; rather, they tapped into something deeply nomadic in him—something that went beyond competition to embrace, as he put it, "that sense of being completely off the grid."

They married in 2005, and at home Carmichael was a devoted, even conventional husband, running the business he founded—La Colombe Torrefaction, a high-end coffee roaster and retailer—and accompanying his wife to Philadelphia Flyers games, where she sings the national anthem. She missed him when he left on long treks, but she didn't try to stop him. A cancer survivor, Hart knew what it meant to reach exhaustion and press on. After Carmichael failed in his first Antarctic attempt, it was his wife who encouraged him to set out again.

He did it with another loved one in mind. His grandfather, a World War II pilot, had painted *"Tout Jour Prest,"* Old French for "always ready," on his plane. Carmichael had the phrase tattooed on his right arm.

The temperature was 35 below zero when Carmichael began his trek. At Hercules Inlet, the starting point, he duct taped his cheekbones and nose to soften the impact of frost and wind. He pulled on his wool Flyers cap and goggles, strapped on cross-country skis, and harnessed Betty the Pig to his shoulders. He glanced at his marine compass, his main navigational tool, which he secured below his chin by soldering quarter-inch copper pipes into a kind of metal bow tie. Then he set off.

The first incline ran unrelenting for fifty-seven miles, the slope intensifying the impact of 65 mph gusts that could knock the air out of your lungs. The wind had sculpted snow and ice into formations called sastrugi, sometimes as tall as a man, sometimes as wide as a ship. Otherwise, there was nothing to see—just a vast, barren landscape.

Eight miles in, Carmichael's ski binding broke, then a ski pole. Calling off the trek at that point would have made sense. He had never planned to *walk* to the Pole.

But he couldn't quit. From age 17, when he'd traversed Washington's Columbia Basin desert for a week by himself, to dozens of other solo treks across forbidding routes through the Sahara and Saudi deserts, he'd conceded defeat only once, in Antarctica.

"I've come so far, and I'm never going to get another shot," he told the video camera he brought to record and verify the journey. He was disheartened—but still determined to beat the record.

Tout jour prest.

Within two weeks, he was fifty miles behind McKeand's pace. He recalibrated, increasing his daily schedule from seven to ten 70-minute marches—a goal of 19.7 miles per day—to make up the deficit. In business, Carmichael believed the key to success was sticking to a plan without compromise. If you let yourself slip, laxness would defeat you.

"You can never stray from your routine," he said. "If you rely on adrenaline or emotion, you burn out. Inspiration comes from doing the work, not as a catalyst to do the work."

But keeping to a plan isn't always possible, and it didn't take long for some of Carmichael's worst fears to materialize. In Antarctica, nature itself lays traps. Tiny shards of ice collect on one side of a crevasse until they bridge the gap, creating a solid-looking veneer hiding a seemingly endless blue abyss. Carmichael stepped on one such bridge only to feel the ground yawn beneath his feet. He caught himself on one side of the ledge, held on tight, and pulled himself up.

It was the closest he'd ever come to losing his life. And it was only his fourth day out.

Problems accumulated like falling snow. A neoprene veil

he'd attached to his goggles stiffened into a board of frost and rubbed the skin off his nose. His cheeks swelled from the cold as though he'd been to a bad dentist.

On day seven, in whiteout conditions, Carmichael arrived at a long tract veined with crevasses. He wouldn't have had a problem crossing them on skis—but on foot, it was treacherous. He checked in with Patriot Hills, the base camp, using his satellite phone. "Do not move," they told him. "Absolutely do not move."

Carmichael took stock of his position relative to McKeand's record. I'll take that advice under consideration, he thought to himself, and pressed on.

Now he was covering at least nineteen miles a day. Once, he went 26.6 miles, thought to be the longest anyone has trekked in Antarctica in a single day. His agony was matched by surges of joy, when he believed he was doing what he was put on earth to do.

"The object of life is not to avoid pain," he said into the camera. "Beautiful things sometimes require pain, and this is one of them." Another time he contemplated how he kept going. "I think, it could be worse," he said. "I think of my wife. She survived non-Hodgkin's lymphoma, a year of chemotherapy. That's a lot worse than this."

He had another reason to be positive. He and Hart were in the process of adopting a six-year-old Ethiopian girl named Yemi. He was excited about becoming a father.

And life on the ice kept him busy. Via satellite, he'd get text messages from people around the world following his trek. He used every waking minute to read, prep food, set up his tent.

When it was time to rest, he'd zip himself into his cocoon sleeping bag, cover his eyes to block out the 24-hour light, and sleep until his alarm went off. Then he'd scarf down 1,000 calories of porridge and 850 calories of chocolate-mint patties and sausages. Food kept him warm. Eating every time he took a break, with big meals at breakfast and dinner, he ingested 8,000 calories a day. But he burned 12,000, a deficit that caused him to lose more than a pound a day.

Determination and discouragement ebbed and flowed. By day twenty-seven, Carmichael was heavy with doubt. His face was battered, and he had burn marks under his eyes.

"I'm beginning to question whether it's physically possible to do this," he said to the camera. In vast fields of snow, he sank to his knees with each step. The constant plunging and lifting was like being on a StairMaster for fourteen hours a day.

On day thirty-five, he was still twenty miles behind McKeand's pace. Yet the record would soon be the least of his worries.

About eighty miles from the Pole, Carmichael's GPS broke. His compass would only point him to the magnetic pole, hundreds of miles from his destination—the research station. He needed a more precise measure to be sure of his direction. If he could remember the last position he'd read on the GPS, he might live. If not, he would die.

That wasn't all. His stove gave out, so he had no way to melt snow or hydrate food. He wanted to speak with his wife, but his satellite phone was dead. He reached for the backup to find that it, too, was useless.

He thought of Robert Falcon Scott, the British polar explorer who in 1912 had perished, along with his team, 11 miles from safety. "I'm two days away from the Pole. No one knows where I am. There's a small possibility I could die out here," Carmichael said.

By now his muscles had lost their elasticity and hung from his bones like loose rope. For days he'd been coughing up flecks of blood from "Eskimo lung," frostbite on the lung tissue.

That's when the hallucinations began. He saw his relatives, and the station appeared as a speck in the distance. Was it there? Was it two miles away—or ten?

The Pig carried his tent and all his supplies. It had kept him alive, and he'd become as emotionally attached to it as a toddler to a blanket. But now it was a millstone. He unhooked it.

He took only his camera, started off, hesitated, turned back. Without the Pig, his sense of isolation was total and profound. He willed himself on. Whenever he lost sight of the station, he'd turn to check his tracks and make sure he wasn't walking in circles.

And then, on December 21, having trekked forty-seven straight hours, he stepped up onto the wide airstrip of the South Pole station.

Inside, they'd known Carmichael was coming but weren't sure when he'd arrive. A woman came out and waved to him. She pointed to the ceremonial pole, which he touched as he verified his time. He'd broken the record: 39 days, 7 hours, and 49 minutes, less than two hours ahead of McKeand.

Carmichael was elated. But he knew he looked bad and

sounded confused. He told the woman who greeted him that he had to go back out to the ice: "I have to get the Pig." She didn't understand, but he was too exhausted to explain. She took him inside.

"What can we do for you?"

"I'd just like something to eat," Carmichael said.

After more than a month of 4,000-calorie-a-day deficits, he felt as if his brain were out of gas. He could smell eggs and maple syrup on a big buffet nearby. He hadn't had a proper meal in almost six weeks.

"I'm sorry," she told him, "but we can't feed tourists."

"I just need calories," he said. "Just give me some condiments and I'll be fine. I just need some sugar."

But the station policy was strict: Provisions were for authorized personnel. The station gets about one hundred visitors a season, mostly wealthy tourists who fly in to stand next to the ceremonial pole, take a photo, and depart. A handful of trekkers on expedition teams come in, almost all of them through a club called Ski Last Degree, which arranges treks from the 89th to the 90th degree south latitude, a sixty-nine-mile journey. And eight or ten hard-core trekkers—the sort of people who, like Carmichael, regard Everest as a glorified Disney World—arrive every year in small groups. They, like anyone who comes through, are required to be self-sustaining.

Carmichael had arranged to have Patriot Hills drop supplies, and they had arrived as planned. But he didn't know where they were and didn't have the strength to pull the box apart anyway. He was also battling to breathe.

He convinced the woman to ask the station manager to make an exception. While she was gone, a kitchen worker who had heard the exchange gave him two big cookies piled with frosting, which he wolfed down. Then he went out to the tent that the station provides for visitors, who aren't allowed to sleep inside the buildings. He curled up on the icy floor and fell asleep.

By now the staff realized that Carmichael wasn't a tourist and needed help. When the station manager found him coughing up quantities of blood in his sleep, the medical staff rushed to act. Carmichael could see the panic in their eyes as they looked at an X-ray of his lungs. They started him on a nebulizer. It took forty-eight hours to get his lung capacity to fifty percent.

"He was lucky," says Wayne Moore, the physician assistant who treated Carmichael. "I think he had maybe 24 hours to live. His airway would have swollen to the point where he wouldn't have been able to move air."

Carmichael's timing was also fortunate. "The next day, visibility went down to a quarter mile and stayed like that for days," Moore says. "There was no way he would have seen the station."

Everyone at the station wanted to see Carmichael. Once he was stable, he offered to give a talk about his experience to the staff. "I thought five or six people would come," he recalls. More than 150 showed up.

The road to recovery was longer than his four days at the station and the three days to get back to Philadelphia. A few weeks later, his skin was still burned, and he was still twenty pounds underweight. But that was okay. He had achieved a goal that had obsessed him.

When asked what motivated him on the ice, he talked about the paradox of being self-reliant while also needing other people. The hundreds of text messages he received, many from people who'd survived cancer or other challenges, helped keep his spirits up.

"On one hand, I felt like I couldn't fail in front of all these people who were counting on me," he says. But then, thinking about what they'd overcome inspired him too. "Inspiration is like love. It's something you get in proportion to what you give."

Soon he would give—and receive—even more. When Hart met him at the airport in Philadelphia, she had news of their daughter. "Yemi," she told him, "will be ours in a few months."

Tout jour prest, he thought. Always ready.

TERROR ON THE CLIFF

BY KENNETH MILLER

Ogtooth Peak, in Central California's Sierra National Forest, towers 10,300 feet above sea level, jutting from the surrounding rock like a hand reaching for the sky. On a Thursday morning last July, three friends eyed the peak and began the ascent from the alpine lakeside where they'd spent the second night of a camping trip. The group, all experienced hikers, wasn't daunted by the two-mile stretch up gradually rising switchbacks to the peak's base. But the last 200- to 300-yard trudge toward the summit was a different story.

When the trio rounded a bend and saw the rocky ascent to the peaks, the eldest of the trio, 72-year-old Birde Newborn, turned back. She suffered from heart trouble and didn't want to push her limits. Her companions, Larry Bishop and Cerena Childress, made it another hundred yards to the last dip before Dogtooth's jutting apex. They paused beneath a wind-twisted cedar to contemplate the final hundred-yard stretch, which required a scramble over massive boulders.

106

To Bishop, a retired hazardous-materials specialist for the Santa Barbara County Fire Department, the challenge seemed minor. At 64, he was lean and vigorous. He'd been hiking, on and off, since he was a Boy Scout; in recent years, after returning to the hobby, he'd bagged some of the highest peaks in the West. Compared with 14,000-footers like Mount Whitney or Mount Langley, he thought, this was nothing.

Childress, 67, was a passionate outdoorswoman, the most seasoned member of the informal backpacking club she'd cofounded with Newborn and Bishop at their church. Still, she wasn't as limber as she used to be. "Those rocks look like leg breakers," she said when Bishop asked if she was coming. "Anyway," she added, nodding toward her Tibetan spaniel, which was snuffling through the chaparral, "Clover wouldn't make it. I'll wait here."

Bishop removed his day pack so that it wouldn't upset his balance on the uneven terrain. "I'll run up and take a few pictures. Back in no time."

"Give a yell if you find that easier trail we saw online," Childress said. "Or if you break your leg."

Bishop laughed and strode off, swinging his hiking poles. The website they'd consulted for the trip had mentioned an alternate route to the peak, but there was no sign of it as he clambered through the boulder field. It took him just fifteen minutes to reach the jagged mountaintop, where a group of Outward Bound instructors and students were practicing rappelling. He joined them in admiring the gorgeous panorama of the High Sierras. He cupped his hands and shouted to Cerena to join him. He heard no response.

As he started down, Bishop noticed a cairn—a pile of stones often used to mark a trail. Was this the easy way? He headed in the direction the cairn seemed to indicate.

The path down from the summit quickly grew steeper. There were no more markers, but Bishop saw a flat, sandy patch about thirty feet below; perhaps it led to an outlet. Soon the slope was nearly vertical, and he had to face the rocks and use his hands to lower himself.

Then his foot slipped, and he was sailing through the air. Dazed, he lay in the sand, trying to piece together what had happened. He'd fallen only ten feet, and no limbs were broken. But when he touched the back of his head, his hand came away bloody. Bishop pulled some paper towels from his cargo pocket and stuffed them inside his broad-brimmed hat to cover the wound. He considered calling to the Outward Bound group, but he wasn't badly injured. And he was confident that he could find his way down.

This trail, he now realized, wasn't so easy after all; in fact, it didn't even seem to be a trail. Climbing back up would be too dangerous. But if he descended a bit farther, he figured, he could navigate around the base of the peak to where Childress was waiting. He began to follow a narrow drainage channel down the mountainside. Soon it led him to a vast expanse of granite, as steep and slick as a playground slide, which emptied onto a boulder field six hundred feet below. Bishop tried using the edge of a slab for traction, but his boots shot out from under him, and he skidded a short yet terrifying distance on his backside. He tried again—and skidded again.

Just below him was a shallow depression in the rock. He

scuttled gingerly down to it, wedged his butt into the crevice, and planted his hiking poles in two small cracks to hold himself in place.

Clinging to the side of the mountain, he began to fully understand his predicament. He'd left his cell phone in his tent, but there was no reception out here anyway. He had an emergency whistle, but it was in his day pack, along with his water bottle, granola, and jacket. The sun beat down through the thin mountain air, and he was already thirsty. He shouted for help, but the only response was the echo of his own voice.

Fishing in his pockets, Bishop found a few mints, his camera, his datebook, and a pen. He popped a mint into his mouth to fight the dryness, then took a photo of the landscape and another of his own face. It was 2 p.m. In the datebook, he wrote to his wife and their 30-year-old daughter, beginning, "Kal and Sarah, I love you. Sorry I can't make it."

Then he explained how he'd gotten into this mess. If someone found him at the bottom of the cliff, he wanted his family to know what had happened.

At the base of Dogtooth Peak, Cerena Childress was recovering from a nosebleed, probably brought on by the altitude. More than an hour had passed since she thought she heard Bishop calling her name from somewhere above, and there was still no sign of him. She didn't dare try to reach the summit to look for him, and there was no one else to ask for help—she hadn't seen another hiker in ages.

Around 1 p.m., she noticed that Clover's paw was bleeding. She would have to carry him back to camp, and the going would be slow. Maybe Larry is lying out there hurt, Childress thought; if so, my sitting here won't do him any good. Or maybe he decided to go have an adventure. In any case, she needed to get back to camp before dark.

When she reached the campsite two hours later, she learned that Birde Newborn hadn't seen Bishop either. It was too late to hike out and alert the authorities.

Larry Bishop felt relieved as shadows covered the rock face and the heat grew less brutal, but as the temperature dropped into the fifties, he began to shiver. Periodically, he shouted for help, mostly to hear the sound of someone's voice. Each time an airplane passed, he experienced a surge of hope—could they be searching already?—then a rush of disappointment. In his datebook, he scribbled observations ("Facing death, the world sure looks beautiful"), regrets ("If only I'd brought my jacket"), resolutions ("I will cherish water"). To minimize his own suffering, he remembered that of others: his older sister, who struggled with emphysema; the migrant workers he'd met forty years before, as a Peace Corps volunteer in Borneo, who faced hunger daily and carried all their possessions on their backs.

Sleep, he knew, would be fatal—if he let his limbs go slack, he would slide six hundred feet down the mountain. So as darkness fell, he began to sing every song he knew: Beatles songs, folk songs, lullabies he'd sung to his daughter when she was a baby. The lyrics to "Help Me Make It Through the Night" took on a special urgency. He watched the constellations wheel overhead and tried to remember all their names. To keep warm and ward off muscle cramps, he did tai chi exercises, moving his arms and legs as much as his awkward position permitted.

Still, by the time the eastern sky grew pink, he was sore in every part of his body. At 5:30 Friday morning, he wrote the day's first journal entry: "Survived until sunrise."

Around the same time, Cerena Childress and Birde Newborn were watching the first rays filter through the fabric of their tents. Neither had slept much. The evening before, they'd learned from a fellow camper that the closest place to make a phone call was at Courtright Reservoir, a nine-mile march eastward through rugged backcountry. As the faster hiker, Childress volunteered to make the journey. She set out at 7:30 a.m.

Newborn—leading Clover—headed for the trailhead they'd started from, five miles to the west, where Bishop's car was waiting in the parking lot. (Fortunately, he'd left behind a set of keys.)

At 12:30 p.m., after taking a wrong turn that led to a six-mile detour, Childress stumbled up to the caretaker at Courtright Reservoir and gasped out her story. The woman called the Fresno County Sheriff's Department on the nearby power station's satellite phone. By late Friday afternoon, Childress and Newborn were sitting by the trailhead, watching searchers assemble to hunt for their friend.

Around 10:30 a.m., Bishop decided to move to another dimple in the rock, thirty feet below, whose dimensions appeared more comfortable. He calculated that he could reach it by rolling onto his belly, then using his hiking poles to make a controlled slide. But the instant he rolled over, gravity took hold. He sped past the hole, accelerating for three hundred feet, until his feet rammed into a small ridge.

Heart pounding, he lay there for several minutes, then checked himself for damage. Incredibly, his limbs were still intact, though the skin was rubbed raw over much of the front of his body and face, and his elbows were painfully bruised. His pants were shredded, too, and he'd lost his wallet and his hiking poles. Slowly, Bishop edged down another fifty feet, stopping at a small hole where purple-flowered plants were growing. He chewed on a stem, hoping for some moisture, but it only made him thirstier.

Bishop continued on to the lowest possible resting place, a dent in the granite that was just deep enough to cradle his hip, with a foothold below it and a handhold above. From there, the slope ran its last unobstructed three hundred feet into the boulder field.

Around 3 p.m., he saw a helicopter buzz by and was gripped with despair when it didn't slow down. Then, to his astonishment, he spied something beyond the boulders that he hadn't noticed before: an abandoned ski lift. There were tents scattered among the pylons, a man painting at an easel, an SUV. Elated, Bishop waved and yelled, but when he looked again, it had all vanished—there were only pine trees.

He realized he'd been hallucinating, his senses deranged by dehydration and sleeplessness. Two hours later, though, he saw three beige helicopters circling, with men in sunglasses gazing down at him. He gestured frantically and shouted himself hoarse. They disappeared, and again he realized his grasp on reality had lapsed.

Finally, at 7:15, Bishop saw a Fresno Sheriff's Department chopper cruise slowly past. He was absolutely certain this one was real—and this time, he was right. But in his drab clothes, against the expanse of gray rock, he was an invisible speck. The pilot never saw him.

On Friday night, three Sheriff's deputies hiked into the wilderness with Fresno County Search and Rescue Mountaineering Team volunteers. They scoured the mountains until well past midnight, by the light of headlamps and lanterns. Then, just after dawn on Saturday, they went searching again. Childress, who'd slept in the car with Newborn, joined the effort that morning, breaking her hand in a fall along the way.

In the afternoon, one party ran into the Outward Bound group that had met Bishop on Dogtooth Peak. After learning that he'd headed down the eastern side of the summit, the searchers concentrated their efforts there. Around 4 p.m., Deputy David Rippe—a 30-year-old detective with the Internet Crimes Against Children Task Force—was combing the base of the peak when he heard what sounded like a moan.

"Did you hear that?" he asked the deputy beside him.

The deputy, Greg Villanueva, nodded. Then he pointed to the cliff face and exclaimed, "Hey, I see him!"

A tiny figure was dangling from the rock, clearly struggling to hold on.

Bishop had managed to stay alert through his second night on the rock, but as the day wore on, he couldn't stop himself from dozing. Each time he awoke, he found he'd slipped down to a spot where only one foot and one hand could grip the wall. He kept dragging himself back up to his precarious refuge, but the effort was growing increasingly difficult.

Finally, he slipped into a dream: He saw a giant clock with a single hand, which was ticking backward toward zero. He understood that zero was death, and the only way to stop the hand from getting there was to resist the urge to relax.

A new thought occurred to him: Maybe if I let go, I can survive the fall. But before he could give it more thought, he saw men in orange vests running toward the bottom of the cliff.

Plotting a safe route up three hundred near-vertical feet of slippery granite takes careful consideration. Deputy Rippe didn't have time for that. Instead, he yelled for everyone to stay away from the area directly beneath Bishop. Rippe shouted for one volunteer to come with him, then scrambled upward. Behind him, ambulance-company manager Russ Richardson—leader of the search-and-rescue volunteers—rocketed up a different route. Rippe's trajectory was more accurate, and within minutes, he was crouching on a ledge directly above Bishop. The hiker's leg was shaking with strain, and he was covered in scrapes and bruises.

"I'm here," Rippe said. "I've got you. You're safe."

That wasn't entirely true. First, Rippe had to move Bishop to the ledge where Rippe was perched, a task that put both men at risk of tumbling off the cliff. To lessen that possibility, Rippe improvised a sling, threading a length of webbing between Bishop's legs and looping it around a knob in the rock. Pinning the loose end with his knee, Rippe grabbed Bishop under the arms, hoped for the best, and pulled.

An instant later, they were sitting side by side. His throat so parched he could barely speak, Bishop croaked out thanks as profusely as he could.

"Have you been in that position all this time?" the deputy asked. Bishop tried to answer, but he'd used up the last of his strength.

A helicopter flew Bishop to a Fresno hospital, where he was treated for abrasions and dehydration; he was discharged that evening. He spent the night with Childress and Newborn in a nearby motel. The next morning, his wife, Kal, drove four hours from Buellton to bring him home.

She did some lecturing, but she knew that the same determination that had helped lead her husband into danger had kept him clinging to the cliff. Bishop himself is thankful for many things—beginning with the searchers who found him as his clock was running out. He has learned a few lessons too: "Don't be so impulsive. Realize I have limits."

Deputy Rippe came away with a different kind of insight. This was the first time he'd found a missing hiker alive who was in a predicament like Bishop's.

"Usually, by the time we get there, it's a body recovery," he explains. "This shows you to never give up hope. Anything is possible."

KILLER WAVE

PETER MICHELMORE

It takes a massive disturbance to create a monster wave. And in the Gulf of Alaska two low-pressure systems collide, creating a mammoth storm. Sustained winds blow southward over hundreds of miles of open ocean, fetching up huge swells.

Eighteen hundred miles south of the gulf, off the headland of Pillar Point, California, lies a shallow undersea rock shelf. It's a famous break called Maverick's, known to surfers for kicking up some of the biggest waves in the world—and the swells are headed directly for it.

"It's coming," the voice on the other end of the line said. "When are you getting up here?" Shawn Alladio knew what the caller meant.

"How big?" she asked. "Is it worth it?"

"B-I-G," her surfer friend told her.

It's a surfing fantasy to ride a hundred-foot wave. But in order to catch waves over forty feet, surfers need someone to tow them—they simply can't paddle fast enough to catch these huge, swift-moving walls of water. They need someone on a fast watercraft to help—and Shawn Alladio is that expert.

Within hours of getting the call on November 14, 2001, Alladio went to a warehouse in Desert Hot Springs, California, and got her water rescue equipment: towlines, tools and medical supplies. She loaded four new WaveRunners on a 30-foot trailer hitched to a weathered, old white Ford truck, and headed north on a 12-hour drive to Pillar Point.

Maverick's is the Everest of surfing. Since the '70s, a few of the elite have ridden waves as high as 60 feet there. A maverick herself, Alladio wanted to be with them. At 18 she'd bought her first Jet Ski and discovered she was good on it. So good that she began teaching lifeguards in Los Angeles harbor. Not that she necessarily got respect. There were always the guys who referred to her as "a dumb blonde." That didn't deter her. She worked hard building her skills—and became one of the leading trainers in the country.

So expert she led schools for Navy Seals and the Coast Guard's rescue swimmers. One of the few women in a very macho world, Alladio, 40, now spent fifty weeks a year on the road living out of her truck. She drove from Daytona Beach, Florida, to Lake Havasu City, Arizona, to the Pacific Coast giving watercraft operation and water-safety lessons. Once she got to Pillar Point, Alladio began tuning up her WaveRunners for safety patrols.

Excitement was building among surfers tracking the swells coming south. Alladio saw a lot of familiar faces, many of the same guys she had taught towing. Training with her this time was a stocky college kid, Jonathan Cahill, who planned to be a watercraft instructor.

Alladio knew the best could be impulsive. They over-reached. Some didn't like being taught by a woman. But in the water, she was in charge. If they were going to be in the surf together, she hoped Cahill understood that.

On Tuesday, November 20, a moored buoy 600 miles out from the Oregon coast was recording 50 m.p.h. winds stoking swells that averaged forty-two feet and passed every twenty seconds—twice as long as those in calm weather. This signified waves of immense volume and power—and they still had 750 miles to grow before reaching Maverick's.

At six a.m. on Wednesday, stormy, gray-green waves were cresting twenty feet high. On the beach, men were wrestling into wet suits, while others were already paddling ten-foot boards across a lagoon. They threaded through jagged sandstone rocks and out into the ocean to line up at the break a half-mile offshore. The waves at this point were running thirty feet.

One by one, the less skilled surfers began to paddle off to the shoulders of the brutal surf. Straddling their boards, they watched the experts ride through slate-colored tunnels forty and fifty feet high. Men began to wipe out. Boards were smashed and bodies bruised. One surfer hurtled through the rock outcroppings and barely survived.

Alladio was at work in the harbor, her hair tied back in a ponytail, when one of the regulars came by with a broken board.

"You'd better get out there," he told her. "It's doubling. Somebody's gonna die in the next thirty minutes."

She went. Steering her nine-foot, blue-and-white jet craft through the harbor entrance, a 150-yard gap in a long jetty wall of volcanic boulders, Alladio saw turbulence tearing kelp from the seabed. If she hit a patch, the seaweed would be sucked into her machine's jet pump and she'd be dead in the water. Dead.

Turning north to the break, she began ferrying in exhausted surfers. On her fifth trip she watched a frigate-sized wave sweep a man off his board and slam him against the rocks. Alladio sped there, grabbed and hauled him aboard, battered but alive.

Minutes later, mounting seas surged over the jetty and caught a group of spectators off guard. Two were washed into the harbor. Alladio and other harbor patrol craft had to do some dangerous maneuvering to fish them out. It always amazed her how people underestimated the ocean. Someone, she feared, might indeed die today.

In the early afternoon a stiffening wind whipped the ocean into sixty- to seventy-foot waves. Reluctantly, even the best surfers retreated to the harbor. The channel was a turbine of white water. Waves were crashing over the jetty when Alladio decided to head outside the break once more to patrol for incoming boats.

As she left the boat ramp, Jonathan Cahill arrived and asked if he could go with her. Considering the risks, Alladio finally told him he could take one of her WaveRunners.

"If you make it to the outside, you've got to stay with me," she said. "Stay within twenty-five feet of my shoulder."

Cahill put on a wet suit, fired up the watercraft and punched through the surf to join Alladio. Out beyond Maverick's wild water, they rocked on high rolling swells, guarding the harbor—watching for craft heading for safety, unaware of the treacherous surf that blocked the entrance. The dark sky was filled with racing clouds. Alladio edged her jet closer to Cahill.

"Over six billion people in the world," she said, "and we are the only ones with all this beauty in front of us."

A moment later she glanced northwest. A high gray wall obliterated the horizon. At first Alladio thought it was a fog bank. But white water was feathering off the top. It was a wave—one hundred feet high—coming at them with the speed of a train. For a heartbeat Alladio thought they could outrun it. Then she knew they couldn't. In calm water her WaveRunner had a maximum speed of 65 m.p.h., but not in these seas. If they turned and ran, they'd be overtaken and buried.

There was only one thing to do. Go over it. Charge up the towering face of the wave and try to get to the crest before it toppled and crushed them. It was probably impossible. It was also their only chance.

"Go! Go! Go!" she yelled to Cahill, pointing at the wave. Would he listen? Such a move was entirely counterintuitive. Fear and instinct said flee. Would he stay with her? Do exactly what a woman told him? His life depended on it.

The wave front was not smooth; there was too much energy in it. It was rough-skinned, a shape-shifting monster new and terrifying every inch of the way. Such a wave does not spill over you like a shower. It avalanches like cement poured off a building. It can snap your neck, break your back, pull you down in an alligator death roll and hold you there. A big wave drowns you and then drags your body over the reef to tear you to pieces.

Standing, leaning forward over the handlebars in a racing stance, Alladio charged the wave. She pushed her jet to full throttle. The wave kept rising until it towered over her, high as a ten-story building. Then she hit the base and started climbing its face.

Water actually rushes up the front of a lifting wave, and Alladio had the sensation of rocketing upward and slipping back at the same time. A single mistake, the slightest hesitation, and she and Cahill would be dead. She had half a second to glance to her left. He was following! Out of the corner of his eye, Cahill glimpsed Alladio's white helmet and fought to keep up with her.

As they made the top of the climb, they both eased off the throttle. Too much speed over the lip, and they'd fly right off the machine. Cahill was mirroring her every move. Everything was happening at once. At the crest, Alladio checked the horizon—and saw the train. Four more waves even bigger were booming toward them. Waves come in sets—and these looked like mountains on the move. They'd just have to go up and over them all.

A second later, as they started down the backside, she heard a crack like thunder as the wave broke in an avalanche of water. They had made it over just in time. Cahill had a stricken look on his face. She willed him to stay with her. They roared down the trench between liquid canyon walls, straight into the next wave. Her craft shuddered as she pulled hard at the

throttle to regain speed. But through a curtain of spray she saw
that this wave was breaking in a direction opposite the first.
Quickly she zigzagged to correct course.

To add to the danger, the wave was raking the bottom, cutting through seaweed like a scythe. If their jet pumps sucked
in kelp and the engines died—they died. She put it out of her
mind, and sped on.

At the north side of the headland, people were scrambling
along the cliffside path when the first wave swept through the
lagoon. It surged up the slope, stampeding the trail. Two-ton
boulders were blasted off the jetty and a steel marker buoy was
torn from the ocean floor. The harbor looked like it had been
hit by a hurricane.

Out at sea, Alladio and Cahill were jerked up by the second
wave. Foaming, bumpy water covered its cliff-size surface. Then
they shot over the wave's lip, first soaring into the air, then free-
falling down the backside. Yet another charged at them—and
another. Down in the trough, the fifth wave looked vertical,
peeling top to bottom down the line in an enormous barrel.

Her heart thumping, Alladio took off up the face at a 45-de-
gree angle. Cahill was right behind her. Up, up they went, racing for their lives to beat the peel. The sound was like Niagara.
Bullet-like spray fired off the crest. Then they were airborne.
Stalling in space. Falling free. Hitting the backside of the wave,
they plunged elbow-deep into the rolling sea. It was over.

The train had passed through. Alladio shut off power and
clutched her head in her hands. She was shaken to the core—
and grateful. Then she and Cahill began yelling at the top

of their lungs, just yelling at the sky. Finally, they retreated to shore. But not for long. Alladio knew she should face the waves, not fear them. Heart still pounding, she climbed aboard her WaveRunner and set out to guard the harbor—and test the ocean's power once more.

THE
WRONG PLACE
AT THE
WRONG TIME

JET CRASH IN THE JUNGLE

LYNN ROSELLINI

"Let's do something different," Monica Glenn said to her fiancé, William Zea, shortly after he proposed. "Let's honeymoon in the jungle."

Monica, an American from California, had met William in Arequipa, Peru, where she was teaching English in an elementary school. The two sang in a choir at the local university. She was a soprano. William, who was working toward a professional degree in industrial engineering, was a tenor. The romance bloomed to the strains of the haunting Spanish folk song "Te Quiero" ("I love you").

Their wedding, on August 21, 2005, was picture-perfect. Monica swept down the aisle of the old Peruvian church in a handmade gown, clutching a bouquet of melody roses and beaming at her family, who'd flown in from California to be there. Two days later, the newlyweds rattled along a winding coastal road on a fourteen-hour bus ride to Lima, spinning with excitement.

A 27-year-old with a sweep of shoulder-length brown hair,

Monica had always been an adventurer. After college, she joined the Peace Corps and taught English in a rural village in China. Still eager to explore new cultures, she found a teaching position—and William—in Arequipa. As the bus bumped along, Monica flipped through a guidebook, reading about the Peruvian rain forest, one of the most biodiverse places on earth.

"I hope we see some monkeys," she said to William.

They planned to fly to the northeast city of Pucallpa, and then on to Iquitos, a frontier town at the headwaters of the Amazon. The area was known for its hanging bridges—catwalks constructed high up in the treetops of the jungle—and for its wilderness river cruises. Their tour package included a four-day trip down the Amazon in a shallow-draft boat. Sleeping in single beds surrounded by mosquito netting in a jungle lodge isn't everyone's dream honeymoon—but it was theirs. A real adventure.

At the airport in Lima, another American, Gabriel Vivas, was on an excursion of his own. Gabriel, a round-faced man with a crew cut and a big smile, stood on the tarmac, waiting to board the red-and-white TANS Peru jetliner. With him, gripping a carry-on and a shopping bag filled with gifts, was his wife, Diana. The two Brooklyn residents had saved to make the trip from New York—their first vacation away from their five kids. They had planned to fly to Pucallpa so Diana could finally meet Gabriel's dad.

"It's just a hop, skip and a jump," Gabriel, the manager of an audio-equipment rental store, told Diana, who was a nervous flier.

The trip was special in another way. Accompanying them

were Gabriel's brother, José, and his three girls. José's oldest daughter, Joshelyn, was celebrating her fifteenth birthday, or Quinceañera—which in Latin countries marks a girl's transition from childhood to maturity. There was going to be a family party with music, dancing, and a five-layer cake with pink roses. Now, laden with backpacks, CDs and forty-five treat bags for local school-children, the Vivas clan jostled up the stairs to board the Boeing 737.

Passengers moved slowly down the aisle, finding seats, stowing luggage, and clicking on seat belts. With ninety-two passengers and six crew members, Flight 204 was filled to near capacity. At 2:24 p.m., the plane lifted off the runway and into sunny skies, then banked over the rooftops of Lima, beginning its climb to a cruising altitude of 33,000 feet. The 300-mile flight would take an hour.

One of the flight attendants, Paola Chu, worked her way down the aisle, serving cake, juice and coffee as passengers leaned toward the windows for a better view. Paola was in charge of the back of the plane. TANS flight attendants took positions based on seniority, and Paola expected to work up front that day. Instead, she was assigned to a second team in the back. She could handle it. In just three short years, flying for two airlines, she'd seen it all—turbulence, unruly passengers, airsick kids.

"Look how beautiful it is!" exclaimed Diana Vivas.

Below lay the Andes mountains, a magical panoply of thickly forested green, laced with shimmering blue rivers and lakes. Next to Diana, Gabriel chatted excitedly, pointing to tiny Indian villages below.

"People there still carry their clothes to the river to wash them," he told his wife.

In the row behind them, the three dark-haired Vivas girls ate cake and sipped soda. Monica Glenn had fallen asleep, but William was awake. The newlywed engineering student was also a volunteer firefighter, and sometimes he found himself replaying images of a 1996 plane crash in the mountains near his hometown. He and his crew had rushed to the site, only to find all 117 passengers dead.

Now he pulled the plastic emergency safety card from the seat pocket and studied it carefully. In case of an emergency, it said, passengers should use the nearest exit. William glanced up; the closest one was two rows in front of him. He put the card back, pushing away his anxiety. The Boeing 737, one of three aircraft owned by TANS Peru, had twenty rows, with four emergency exits: one in the front, one in the middle, and two toward the rear.

The state-owned airline linked Lima with jungle and mountain towns. Flying in remote and rugged regions in poor countries can be risky. The "2005 Safety Report" of the International Air Transport Association shows that the "loss rate" for Western-built jet aircraft is thirteen times greater in Latin America than North America. Adverse weather is a factor in 70 percent of "control flight terrain accidents." That term means the pilot is still at the controls of the plane when it crashes into obstacles, water or the ground. The proficiency of the flight crew figures in fifty percent of such crashes. In January 2003, a TANS plane struck a mountain, killing all forty-six people aboard.

Monica stirred awake and squeezed William's hand.

"It's so green out there!" she said, stretching.

As she gazed down at the lush canopy, the pilot came on the intercom to instruct passengers to fasten their seat belts and to stow tray tables. The plane was making its approach and would be landing in Pucallpa in ten minutes' time. Moments later, as the 737 began its descent, the skies outside darkened. Rain pelted the windows, and the jet began to bump and roll.

Paola Chu had just finished the beverage service and had secured the carts when the "fasten seat belt" sign flashed on. The cabin boss up front called on the service phone and told the flight attendants to take a seat. Paola knew then that the weather was rough. A lighted seat belt sign normally applied only to passengers.

She and her partner took jump seats next to the back door. Unconcerned, Paola checked her makeup in a pocket mirror, expertly applying pink lipstick as the plane bounced and rocked. The turbulence increased, and the plane shook violently. Then there was a stomach-churning drop.

"Oh, my God, my God!" cried Diana Vivas. She grabbed her husband's arm.

"It's okay," he said. "It happens all the time."

But Gabriel was nervous too. Out the window he saw treetops. *Thank God, we're almost down,* he thought. Behind them, Gabriel's nieces were screaming. The plane was bouncing like a ball. White-faced and gripping the armrest, Monica turned to William.

"This isn't right," she said. "Something's wrong."

By now, even Paola was worried. The plane was dropping five

stories, slamming to a stop, then plunging another five stories. Paola couldn't see out the window, but she heard the engines revving loudly, the way they do when a pilot is trying to correct for a landing. She could hear hailstones on the windows.

The plane was out of control, rocking, shaking, hurtling downward. The lights in the cabin flickered out. Paola heard a rapid-fire rat-tat-tat like a stick run against a picket fence—tree limbs at the window! The aircraft shredded its way through a swath of thick rain forest canopy, then slammed to the ground, breaking in half.

In front of Gabriel, seats flew into the air. Oxygen masks popped from overhead. I'll never see my kids again, thought Diana. Gabriel, thrown forward in his seat, felt a gust of heat on his face, as if someone had opened a furnace. He looked up and saw an orange fireball burst in front of him.

"I can't get my seat belt off!" Diana screamed.

The plane was in pandemonium, the aisles dark and filling with thick smoke. Passengers sprang from their seats, surging into the aisle. Their screams added to the confusion. In one swift motion, Gabriel grabbed Diana by the arm, loosened her belt and grabbed his niece Jharline.

"C'mon, move!" he cried, pushing them down the aisle ahead of him. Behind him, he heard a cry: "Ayuda! Ayuda!" A Peruvian woman, trapped by her belt, called for help in Spanish. Gabriel turned back to free her, put her in front of him and said, "Go, go, go." The smoke was so dense, nobody could see.

Some passengers from the front of the plane had struggled down the aisle and were jumping out through the breach at mid-aircraft. William and Monica were out of their seats.

Monica was moving toward the nearest exit, two rows ahead.

"No!" William shouted. "Through the back!"

This contradicted the safety instructions he'd read, but he knew in his gut he was right. The front part of the plane was burning. William pushed his wife toward the rear. As a fire-fighter, he knew most flight fatalities come from victims inhaling hot, toxic gases. Deliberately, he covered his wife's face with his hands.

Paola Chu had been knocked unconscious near the exit at the rear. She woke on the floor of the galley with an excruciating headache, bleeding from a gash in her forehead. The door had burst open on impact, and passengers trampled over her in their rush to get out. Now she struggled to her feet, forcing herself to remember what she'd learned in training: You have just ninety seconds to get the passengers off before the plane explodes.

The exit was now blocked with flames. Paola scrambled to the second rear exit and struggled with the handle. It was stuck. A slight and petite woman, she leaned into it, using all her shoulder, arm and leg strength. She couldn't budge the door.

"Help me," she pleaded. A man assisted, pulling the handle, and Paola gave the door a sharp kick. It snapped open.

"Get out! Get out!" she yelled.

The exit opened into darkness and pelting hail. A murky swamp lay ten feet below. The emergency slide had broken when the plane crashed.

"Jump!" Paola shouted. Passengers hurried toward the exit, pushing and shoving. People were knocked to the floor. Others scrambled over them.

"Don't push," cried Paola. She bent down to help those who'd fallen.

"Don't shove," she ordered. "Get out."

One by one, about twenty passengers leaped out the door and into the swamp. José Vivas and his three girls jumped, then Gabriel and Diana. Monica and William followed them. Smoke and fumes swirled as Paola stood at her post by the door. She was about to black out. Through the din, she heard the screams of passengers still trapped in the plane. They're burning up, she thought. But the black smoke choked her; she couldn't breathe. One more minute in here, she realized, and everyone will die.

Paola moved toward the daylight at the door. Lord forgive me, she thought. And she threw herself from the plane. Outside was a landscape from hell. The plane had cut a quarter-mile swath through the jungle, scattering human bodies, luggage, seats and pieces of fuselage among the broken trees. A woman's body lay partway under the wreckage, long black hair streamed behind her. The body of a flight attendant was tossed amid the debris. Stunned survivors floundered in the mud, while flames licked from the plane, and thick, acrid smoke poured into the air.

Escaping the metal-melting temperatures of the plane, the survivors were startled to find bitter-cold weather. This was not the steaming jungle of the Amazon basin. This was the high rain forest of Peru in the midst of a bone-chilling thunderstorm. Temperatures hovered around freezing, and a driving rain alternated with hailstones as big as marbles. Paola struggled to stand in the waist-high mud. The plane, she knew, could blow up any second.

"Get away from the plane!" she screamed. "Get away!" Many of the survivors had skin blistered from severe burns, and were bleeding from open wounds. Some had lost their shoes in the sucking muck. Thorns tore at their feet and legs as they stumbled toward higher ground. Paola tried to walk, but collapsed. The jump from the plane had torn ligaments in her right ankle. She couldn't walk or free herself from the mud and begged for help. A man, struggling himself, hooked her under the arm and pulled her forward.

A few yards away, Monica was floundering too. Shivering in a T-shirt, light pants and sandals, with her face burned in patches, she was too dazed to be scared. *Is this real or a dream?* she wondered. Next to her, William held his burned hands out in front of him, trying to keep his balance. In using them to shield his wife's face, he'd burned them badly. They were blistered, oozing, the skin shearing off.

A few yards away, he spotted something. Perched alone atop a piece of wreckage near the burning plane was a dark-haired child of eight or nine.

"Mama!" she cried hysterically. "Mama!"

William's heart wrenched. What could he do? As a veteran paramedic with dozens of rescues to his credit, he knew what to do—but with burned hands he couldn't pick her up.

"I'll go," said Monica.

William didn't want her to go. He looked around frantically for help. Another man, a thirty-something Peruvian in a maroon shirt, appeared behind them.

"Please, will you go help that girl?" William begged.

The man waded over, and the child wrapped her arms around his neck. William and Monica scanned the landscape looking for other stranded survivors.

"Is there anyone who needs help?" they yelled. They heard no one. But Gabriel Vivas did.

"What's that?" he asked. He and the rest of his family had made it out and were in the swamp near Monica and William. Gabriel heard a small wail coming from somewhere behind him, closer to the blaze. To a father of five, the sound was unmistakable. It was a child. Turning, he saw a baby lying in the mud some distance away.

"Where are you going?" demanded Diana.

"I'm going back to get that child," Gabriel said. "Keep walking."

Diana was terrified that her husband would be killed when the plane exploded and pleaded with him not to go.

"I'll be okay," Gabriel said as he slogged back toward the fiery wreck.

He was frightened. There was carnage like he'd never imagined. Charred and bloody body parts littered the crash site. If it weren't for the child, he would have turned and fled. In the midst of this desolation, Gabriel found a little boy about a year old. He was barely breathing. His face was cut and bleeding, his body covered with burns. Another passenger had also come to the baby's aid. They would have to act quickly.

With Gabriel at his elbow, the man scooped up the baby, took a few steps and sank waist-high in a swamp hole.

"Let me take him," Gabriel said, gesturing with his hand.

He grasped the baby with one arm and used the other to pull the man free. Carrying the child, Gabriel climbed a hill while the other man cleared a path through the thorny brush. As he plowed through the muck, Gabriel kept watching the child, thinking, *This baby is going to die in my arms! Please God, don't let him die.*

Diana Vivas, frantic with worry, was also praying. She and the rest of the Vivas family had stopped to rest in a jungle clearing about fifty yards from the blazing aircraft. The girls had lost their shoes in the mud and were crying, "Why did the plane crash? When can we go home?"

Diana was shouting into the darkness too.

"Gabby, Gabby!" she called to guide him back.

Paola Chu was in pain, her right foot twice its normal size, her left leg bloody. One eye was swollen shut, and her face was a mass of bruises. Immediately after the crash, an adrenaline rush had pushed her into action. Now, catching her breath as she rested on the wet ground, a wave of emotion crashed over her. What about her friends on the flight crew?

"Where is the rest of the crew?" she asked another flight attendant.

"They are gone," her friend replied.

Paola felt tears coming. Had she served in the front cabin as she'd expected, she'd be dead too. Right now, she had to hold herself together. She still had a job to do. Just then, there was a movement in the brush.

A figure, covered with mud, pushed through the bushes. Gabriel, his face white with strain, staggered forward with a baby in his arms. He laid the child down carefully and asked his brother, José, to tell everyone in Spanish to make a protective circle to shield the baby from hailstones.

A second explosion ripped through the air. Flames flared over the treetops, and the rest of the plane was engulfed. It was too dangerous to stay where they were. Paola decided to get everyone moving to higher ground and to find help. Two men lifted her to her feet, and she urged the passengers to stay together and move farther away from the plane.

"Keep walking," she said. "Stay calm."

Frightened, wet and shaking from the cold, the group plodded on. Gabriel took his sneakers off and put them on his wife's feet. He walked on in his socks, cradling the baby as he went. A man carried Paola. It was still raining, and thunder rumbled in the distance.

Shortly after 4 p.m., the survivors saw two men from a local village approach across an open field. A few minutes later, they spotted the lights of cars. One by one, injured passengers began boarding vehicles bound for hospitals.

Then Gabriel and José saw an unbelievable sight—their father, the person they'd come all these miles to see—had found them. The 67-year-old senior Vivas had been waiting at the Pucallpa airport when he heard about the crash. He rushed to the scene. Now father and sons clung together, swaying from side to side and crying.

The final toll for Flight 204 was forty passengers and crew dead, fifty-eight survivors. An investigation by the Peruvian government attributed the cause of the crash to human error, the pilot having attempted to land in a sudden, violent storm. In Peru, more than half of rural people live on less than $1 a day, and following the disaster, peasants in the area stripped the plane clean of valuables. In no time, the jungle vegetation began to close over the debris. The victims' scars, physical and emotional, were slow to heal.

Paola Chu remained in a Lima hospital for forty days with internal hemorrhaging, edema on the brain and torn ligaments in her right foot.

The baby, Juan Carlos Valle, was treated for burns and a fractured skull. His mother died from injuries, but his father, who was not on the flight, came to take him home.

Monica and William spent their "honeymoon" undergoing burn treatment in a Lima hospital. Although Monica recovered quickly from her injuries, William's severely burned hands took time. Months later, he was still wearing protective gloves.

As for the Vivas family, they escaped serious injuries. Back in New York, the Brooklyn borough president proclaimed "Vivas Family Day," citing the family for "great bravery and fortitude in the face of grave danger." Memories of the horror linger. Loud subway trains now make Gabriel shiver. José hates crowds and going too fast in a car. Diana still has nightmares, and Paola has struggled with depression.

The plane crash made Monica look at her husband and her marriage vows in a new light.

"It's pretty easy to be with someone in the good times," she says. But the notion of sticking together "for better or worse" became very real for her. "The crash put everything to the test," she says. "I made the right choice."

DAM BREAK

WILLIAM H. HENDRYX

A wave of water thirty feet high spun Jerry Toops like a tornado. Debris battered and cut him. He fought to keep his head up, using all the strength in his legs and upper body to swim, angling across the ripping current toward a line of cedar trees.

The night was as black as the water, the trees vague shadows against an ebony sky. As he was swept toward the cedars, Toops grabbed a limb and held on. Wood, pieces of plaster, and litter slammed him, accumulating around his waist like flotsam against a pole in a breakwater. The rubble weighed him down.

He was an outdoorsman with strong, callused hands, but inch by inch, the weight and force of the water pulled his hand down the tree limb, stripping the leaves. Just when he could hold on no longer, the debris gave way, and Toops pulled himself into the swaying treetop. Clinging there, exhausted, wearing only his undershorts in the spitting snow and 32-degree chill, he was limp with fatigue. He was alive, but as he surveyed the rampaging water, he was certain his wife and babies were dead.

Bedtime came early for the Toops family at their three-bedroom brick ranch house nestled in a forested valley in Johnson's Shut-Ins State Park. At 8 p.m. Lisa Toops put the three kids to bed. She and Jerry, superintendent of the park, followed soon after. Self-reliant and religious, they were used to a work cycle that more closely followed the sun than the flow of commuter traffic.

Jerry was a real "ranger type," rugged, fit, good with his hands. His outdoorsman's beard was just beginning to gray at the edges. The 42-year-old naturalist loved the park, with its strange formations of igneous rock called shut-ins. A billion years ago volcanic activity caused a granite upheaval and confined, or "shut-in," the Black River in southeast Missouri. Over the ages, the trapped water carved spectacular gorges, natural water slides, and potholes in the hard rock.

In the summertime, the park was a magnet for swimming, camping and hiking, but now, in the weeks before Christmas, all was quiet. At 4 a.m. that December 14, 2005, the baby awoke, softly crying to be fed. Lisa brushed her sandy hair away from sleepy green eyes, plucked Tucker from his crib near their bedroom and retreated down the hall to the living room sofa to nurse him. Normally, after feeding she'd put him back in his crib, but this night they both fell asleep on the couch.

An hour later, Lisa bolted awake. There was a booming roar—loud, then soft, then loud again—a huge tornado, she thought. She tucked the infant under one arm and jumped up.

"Jerry, get the kids!"

She figured the basement was their only hope. She ran to Tanner's room. The five-year-old was climbing from his bed, awakened by the bedlam. She yelled to him to come, extending her hand, but before she could grasp him, a barrage of water rushed into the house. It coursed around her ankles, her knees. In seconds the water level was above her chest. Lisa held the baby over her head as the surge filled the room. She didn't know what was happening, but tried to stay calm for her kids.

"Hang on to the bed!" she called to Tanner, fighting to stay upright in the flood. The water kept rising, relentlessly.

"Hold your breath, baby!" she called over the din. In the next moment, they were in liquid darkness.

"Jerry—!"

That was all Jerry Toops had heard of Lisa's cry to "get the kids." The sharp urgency in her voice sliced through his sleep a moment before the roar cut off the rest of her sentence. The noise. It sounded like a squadron of jet aircraft flying through the house. Jerry's feet hit the floor, and in that same instant, the back wall of the bedroom exploded, slamming him back. A second later, the opposite wall blew out, heaving him and the bed in reverse. He was deep underwater.

Intuitively, he swam upward—ten feet, twenty, thirty, before surfacing in a sea of uprooted trees, Sheetrock, furniture, and granite boulders the size of SUVs. It looked like the Biblical Flood, everything destroyed. He swam to a portion of rooftop that floated nearby and climbed on.

"Lisa! Tanner! Tara! Tucker!" he called, but couldn't hear

his own voice above the rushing water. Praying to see just one head bob to the surface, he knew the odds were all wrong. He was strong and agile, and it had taken all he had to escape. What chance did they have?

It seemed forever. Underwater, Lisa Toops fought for her life and the lives of Tucker and Tanner. She had no idea where Tara, her three-year-old, was. The thought was terrible. She pushed it aside and focused. As suddenly as it had crested, the water began to recede. Lisa's head came into air. Gasping, she looked up to see the roof splinter and crack open like an eggshell. A way out where there had been none.

She hugged the infant with one arm and swam toward the opening with the other. Where was Tanner? She'd lost her first-born child amid the chaos. Kick your feet, baby, she thought, hoping he would remember the swimming lessons he'd had that summer. Kick your feet. Within moments, she and the infant washed free of the crumbling house, riding what amounted to a tsunami in the wintry pitch of night.

Thirty seconds earlier, he'd been sound asleep. Now Jerry Toops was in a battle for his life. The section of rooftop he'd stood on buckled beneath him, and he dropped back into the swirling waves. Finally, he managed to grab onto the cedar tree and climb from the water. His body was battered and numbed by the freezing chill.

Toops strained his eyes in the dark night. He knew what had happened. He'd foreseen the possibility. He'd even prepared, devising an evacuation plan in case a natural disaster ruptured the dam on the mountaintop less than two miles from their home. His job required it, but his choice to live there had put his family at risk. He blamed himself for their deaths.

Toops was only half-correct about the flood. The dam had ruptured, cascading 1.5 billion gallons—6 million tons—of water into a narrow valley, leveling everything in its path, including an entire hardwood forest. But it was not a natural disaster that released the monster. It was a man-made flaw.

Completed in 1963, the dam had concrete walls ninety feet tall. It was part of the Taum Sauk hydroelectric generating facility owned by the local utility. A fail-safe mechanism had gone awry, allowing the reservoir to overfill. Runoff eroded the soil beneath one edge of the basin, and it crumbled, washing the Toops family away.

Captain Ryan Wadlow of the volunteer fire department in Lesterville was just leaving for his job as a heavy- equipment operator when the emergency pager sounded around 5:50 a.m. Wadlow stood 6'7" and weighed 327 pounds. To strangers he looked threatening; friends and neighbors knew him for his soft heart. Living close by, Wadlow was first on the scene. He didn't know it, but roughly forty-five minutes had elapsed since the Toops family had been swept from their home.

He parked his truck and slogged through knee-deep mud and water, tracing the reflected ruin with his flashlight. Everything in this valley, usually so familiar to him, was unrecognizable. Divested. Scraped away. A stretch of the elevated road was covered in six inches of sludge. A towering wall of uprooted trees had been deposited near the edge of a bridge spanning the Black River. On the opposite side of the roadway from where the family's home had been, several vehicles littered a sodden field as if they'd been dropped from the sky.

Just then, in the silence of predawn, came a faint cry for help. A man's voice, desperate and shaking with cold.

"Where are you?" Wadlow called back.

"Help," was the only reply, repeated again and again.

Shining a path with his flashlight, Wadlow trudged a quarter-mile through light rain and spitting snow into the field, stumbling up to his calves in muck, listening for the voice. Seven minutes later, he found himself under a tree. The voice was coming from above. A man, deathly ashen, wearing only undershorts, was clinging to the upper limbs. He was bleeding and covered with silt and leaves, and appeared to be in shock. Wadlow stretched to his full height, helped Jerry Toops to the ground, and gave him his coat.

"Are you the park superintendent?" he asked.

"Yes," said Toops.

"Anybody with you?" asked Wadlow.

Toops mumbled something unintelligible as Wadlow's two-way radio crackled. Other members of the volunteer department were now on the scene, including Chief Ben Meredith and veteran Gary Maize, looking for survivors. Wadlow escorted Toops to the edge of the flood-scoured field and had another volunteer take him to an ambulance. Then Wadlow returned to search.

Meanwhile, Gary Maize and two others had begun hunting about a half-mile north of Wadlow and the command post.

With one weak flashlight between them, Maize's group inched through a minefield of slimy waste and barbed-wire fences.

"Anybody out there?" Maize shouted. Then he said to the others, "Shhh! I heard something."

He killed his radio and listened intently. Slowly, deliberately, he scanned the field with the light. Just ahead there was something in the rubble. Wearing only a nightshirt, Lisa Toops sat limp and incoherent on the soggy ground near the far perimeter of the field about a half-mile from where her home once stood. She held the gurgling infant tightly to her chest, while five-year-old Tanner lay apparently lifeless across her legs. Neither stirred nor spoke. They had been stranded there in the rain and snow for an hour and ten minutes.

"Ma'am, are you all right?" Maize asked.

Clearly she was not. He took the baby and cleared its air passages of mud and leaves. Another firefighter wrapped Tanner in his coat and felt for a pulse. He couldn't find one. Ryan Wadlow had by now joined the others. He lifted Lisa into his arms and carried her toward rescue vehicles at the edge of the field.

One of the volunteers asked her, "Ma'am, how many children do you have?" Lisa was unresponsive, refusing to let go of Wadlow's neck.

"How many children, ma'am?" Lisa seemed to come awake.

"I have three . . ." she said, and then her voice trailed off into silence. Somehow, in all the tumult, she'd managed to hold on to her baby. And, miraculously, she'd snagged Tanner as he washed by her, crying for help. But she had not seen or heard anything of Tara, her sweet little girl.

After turning Lisa over to volunteers, Wadlow slogged back to the spot where she'd been found. He stood in the stillness for a moment. Then he heard a weak whimper. A child!

He followed the sound. Sloshing through mud, some thirty feet away, he came to a cedar tree. There beneath the boughs, almost invisible under silt and rubbish, lay a little girl in muddy brown pajamas. He came closer and shone his light. Her blue eyes were wide open; her breath came in shallow rasps.

Wadlow swept her up and hurried to the ambulance. Back down the road near the command post, an anguished Jerry Toops was being tended in the other ambulance when word filtered in that they'd "found the baby and little girl." Toops thought that meant their bodies had been found. Dreading the answer, he asked, "Are they alive?"

"Yes," came the reply.

For the first time that night, Jerry Toops wept. The sun rose behind the mountains. Ten minutes later, he learned that Lisa and Tanner were also alive. The family members were gathered like pieces of driftwood and taken to the local medical center. From there, they were transferred to Cardinal Glennon Hospital in St. Louis.

All were suffering from hypothermia and were covered with cuts and bruises—except Tara, who survived without a scratch. Tanner was in the worst shape. An EMT described his condition as "not compatible with life." But the medical team kept working and after almost two hours of CPR, he was revived. Tucker and Tara were hospitalized for six days, Tanner two weeks. Everyone recovered.

ONE INCH FROM DEATH

MICHAEL BOWKER

Thirteen-year-old Dana Bienenfeld sat dejectedly on a rock, frowning as she stared across the boulder-strewn mountainside. None of her classmates or teachers from the River Middle School in Napa, California, were in sight. The steep slope below was a menacing jumble of jagged rocks. In the pine groves beyond that, darkness was already gathering. She felt frustrated and alone.

"Hello!" the dark-haired seventh-grader shouted. "Can anybody hear me?"

No answer. It was June 2, 1997, and Dana's class had just arrived in Yosemite National Park on a year-end outdoor-education trip. After dinner they had hiked up the wooded mountainside.

As Dana's classmates fanned out into the forest, she had picked her way up the rugged slope. She climbed steadily for nearly half an hour before realizing she was alone.

"Help!" she yelled again. "Is anybody around?"

Hearing nothing, Dana's face tightened with anger. *Nobody cares about me,* she thought. Then she caught herself. Throughout sixth grade she had been convinced her classmates disliked her, and spent most of her time alone and depressed. As she entered seventh grade, she vowed to become more outgoing and independent. *I'll just get down on my own,* she told herself.

Dana stepped carefully from rock to rock. The late spring rains had softened the ground in places. After a few minutes she came to a boulder-strewn ledge, fifteen feet across, that tilted back toward the mountain. Dana hopped onto the ledge, landing on a melon-size rock. The rock skidded, and she fell facedown in a shallow depression.

Unhurt, Dana started to get up, but something pushed her back down. An instant later she felt an intense, painful pressure on her legs and back that took her breath away.

Fearing she would suffocate, she fought wildly, gasping for air. As she worked her head around, she was horrified to see that a granite boulder had rolled on top of her. She must have jostled a rock that was holding the boulder in place. Now she was pinned to the earth, able to move only her head, left foot and right hand. Panic-stricken, she tried to yell but managed little more than a whisper.

The boulder, nearly the size of a small car, continued to settle, pushing Dana even deeper into the dirt. She wriggled frantically, pushing up against the great stone, then slowly gave up and lay still. The pain was unbearable. Maybe, she thought, death won't be so bad.

Suddenly the pressure leveled off. The boulder had come to rest—now at least she could breathe. Fear gave way to determination: *Stop thinking about dying and start screaming.* She did, and this time her voice carried up the mountainside.

Less than twenty minutes later, Graham Pierce, administrator of the park's medical clinic, received a signal on his emergency radio. A teacher had heard Dana's cries and alerted a park ranger, who made the call. The 34-year-old Pierce quickly gathered his gear, then, with two members of his medical team, jumped into an ambulance.

As they raced through Yosemite Valley, Pierce grew unusually tense. The report of a possible crush victim brought back a searing memory. Only a few months before, he had been called to a traffic accident. A young man in his twenties, conscious but in severe pain, was trapped under a heavy trailer. Pierce comforted him for more than an hour while they waited for equipment to free him. His vital signs appeared strong, but seconds after the trailer was lifted, he suffered heart failure and died in Pierce's arms.

The experience was still on Pierce's mind when the ambulance reached the base of the mountain where Dana lay trapped. It took him and his team twenty minutes of hard climbing to reach her.

Pierce grimaced when he saw Dana. She lay headfirst on the downhill slope of the ledge, with the boulder covering everything but her legs and head. The five-ton rock teetered over her at an alarming slant. If it rolled even slightly, it would crush her skull. Only the fact that she had fallen into the small depression had saved her.

"This is bad," Pierce said softly to paramedic Kim Ednor as

they hurried to Dana's side. Trapped for almost an hour, she was near hysteria.

"Please get me out!"she shouted.

"We're going to get this rock off you as quickly as we can," Pierce said calmly, checking her pulse. "It's going to take some time, though. You have to be extremely brave. Can you do that?"

She nodded, but Pierce saw fear in her eyes. Keith Lober, director of the park's search-and-rescue team, waved him over. Ednor stayed with Dana.

"We've got a real problem," Lober said. "If we move that boulder just an inch or two the wrong way, it could roll and kill her and anybody near her."

Both men knew Dana's chances of survival were poor. Even if they got her safely from under the rock, she might have already suffered internal injuries.

Pierce cut away Dana's jeans, nearly recoiling at the blue-black color of her legs. He could find no pulse in either of them. The rock was cutting off the blood supply at her waist. If she survives, he thought, she may lose both legs. His breath caught short as he imagined his own daughter in this situation.

Dana cried out as waves of nausea and pain washed over her. Pierce had morphine in his medical kit, but he knew the painkiller would lower her blood pressure. Keeping an even fluid pressure in her body was critical.

Pierce had learned a great deal about crush victims since the death of the man pinned under the trailer. When human cells are torn or crushed, they release large amounts of potassium into the bloodstream. If a heavy weight blocking the blood flow is suddenly lifted, the flood of potassium can cause cardiac arrest.

To help prevent this, the blood pressure must be stabilized through the injection of fluids, which Pierce began administering intravenously. But he had no blood or plasma, so he immediately radioed for the Air Med helicopter, stationed at the Doctors Medical Center of Modesto, more than one hundred miles away.

By now, the girl had been under the boulder for nearly two hours. Pierce talked to her continuously in a confident, reassuring voice. As she listened, Dana shut her eyes and squeezed his hand.

Floodlights illuminated the flank of the mountain where more than thirty rescue workers now labored to free Dana. The surrounding forest was pitch-black. Under Lober's watchful eye, a team carefully drilled holes and attached anchor bolts in the top of the boulder. They then clipped ropes onto the bolts and tied them to trees uphill. Lober hoped these lines would keep the boulder from slipping while they attempted to lift it off Dana.

Another team worked to position the Jaws of Life, a hydraulic tool often used in car accidents. Lober planned to use it like a powerful jack to help lift the rock. Meanwhile, a third team was placing air bags under the boulder. Everything had to be done with absolute precision or the boulder would roll.

Pierce watched Dana's vital signs closely. Her heart seemed strong, but there was still no pulse from her legs.

"We'll have you out of here before long," he told her, smiling. He was glad she didn't know the truth.

Just then, a member of the search-and-rescue team approached Pierce with a worried look. They had found an unstable boulder the size of a bus about seventy-five feet up the mountain, directly above them. *All this activity could cause it to roll*, Pierce thought. *We've got to get her out of here now.*

In a few minutes, everything was in place. At Lober's command, a small amount of air was pumped into the air bags. The boulder rose about a quarter-inch, then began to wobble.

"Hold it!" Lober shouted as the team jammed pieces of wood under the air bags. The rock steadied.

"It's okay," Pierce reassured Dana. "We're getting close to having this thing off you." He stayed by her side, knowing he could not move in time if the boulder rolled.

The operation continued with agonizing slowness. Each time the rock was moved, it teetered on the verge of rolling.

"Hold it! Hold it!" Dana heard the men say over and over. She fought her fear by concentrating on Pierce's voice. "There sure are a lot of people up here who care about you," he told her.

It took nearly an hour to raise the rock one inch. Dana was still wedged tight. Pierce and Lober tried not to think about the unstable boulder up the mountain. It was a cool night, but Pierce's shirt was soaked with sweat.

A short time later, a team arrived with the blood and plasma, which Pierce injected into Dana's arm.

Just before 10:30 p.m., three-and-a-half hours after Dana became trapped, Pierce felt a little give when he gently tugged on her leg. "I think we're close," he told Lober. It was time to go for broke.

Pierce knelt by Dana's side. "We're going to lift the rock

now," he said. "Be brave for a few more minutes, and we'll have you out of here."

Pierce and Lober stationed themselves by her legs. Slowly the crew inflated the air bags. The rock wobbled and began to rise. When it had risen a full inch, the two men looked at each other and nodded.

"Now!" Lober yelled, and they pulled.

"She's moving!" Lober shouted. "She's out!"

Crew members whooped and helped Pierce and Lober lift her away from the boulder. Exhausted, Dana could manage only a smile. She was strapped onto a spine board—used for victims with back and neck injuries—then placed in a Stokes Rescue Basket. The rescue crew had to rope the long metal cage down the steeper parts of the mountain.

Dana watched the stars overhead and was vaguely aware that people were walking beside her.

"Aren't you lucky?" she heard a gentle voice beside her ask. "You get a free ride."

It was almost midnight when they reached the foot of the mountain. An ambulance sped them to Crane Flat, where the Air Med helicopter waited. There was no room on board for Pierce. "I'll see you first thing in the morning," he promised Dana. "You're doing fine."

As the helicopter roared off, Pierce prayed that he was right.

The next morning, Pierce raced up to the second floor of Doctors Medical Center of Modesto. Bracing himself, he opened the door to Dana's room and found her sitting up in bed. She broke into a huge smile.

"You saved my life," she told him. "Thank you." She opened her arms, and the two hugged each other.

Almost miraculously, Dana suffered no broken bones or internal injuries in the ordeal. Her worst injury was a severely bruised and twisted right knee, which took nearly three months to heal.

During her recovery, Dana was visited by dozens of classmates. She also received a huge get-well card signed by the entire school. Two months after the accident, Dana sent Pierce a thank-you card.

"I feel I can face almost anything now," she wrote. "Because nothing under 10,000 pounds scares me anymore."

TWO BOYS, FIVE TONS OF ICE, EIGHTY RESCUERS, AND A CHAIN SAW

JEFF RENNICKE

"Can anybody hear me?" Like everyone else on the mountain that day, firefighter Terry Cushman could feel hope beginning to fade. The golden hour—those sixty precious minutes that give trauma victims the best chance of survival—had long since passed. It had now been three hours since the ice cave in Washington's Cascade mountains had collapsed, leaving two young hikers trapped beneath.

More than eighty search-and-rescue workers from five agencies covered the mountainside near Denny Creek. Using chain saws, shovels, and their bare hands, they had cleared away tons of ice, but tons more remained. So did unanswered questions: Would the victims have enough air to breathe? Would they drown in the rising waters or give in to hypothermia before rescuers reached them? Was it already too late?

Shoving all that aside, Cushman crawled into the shifting ice and yelled again, "Can anybody hear me?" Then he held his breath, straining to hear something—anything—from the frozen rubble below.

Thursday, August 21, 2008, had begun in a flurry of mismatched hiking boots and lost water bottles in the Corbett family's Seattle home. "It was pretty obvious we hadn't done a lot of this," says Joni Corbett, 45, who, with her neighbor Chrissy Gelmini, 54, had planned to take their two sons, two daughters, and two dogs on a day hike in the nearby mountains.

Finally, by early afternoon, the two families were winding their way through the immense spruces and moss-green light of the Denny Creek Trail, fifty miles east of the city. Beside them, the creek chattered with snowmelt. The boys, Alec Corbett, 17, and Alessandro (known as Ollie) Gelmini, 14, ran ahead to explore, while the two girls—Marta Gelmini, 10, and Halle Corbett, 7—stayed closer to their mothers, skipping rocks in the water and playing with the dogs. Beside a small waterfall, they ate the lunch they'd carried in their backpacks.

"It was so pretty and so close to home," says Gelmini. "I remember thinking, *Why don't we do this more often?*"

After lunch, they continued hiking, the trail growing steeper and rockier and the air chillier as they climbed. Two miles from the trailhead, they stopped to watch the creek waters cascade in gauzy sheets down the eighty-five-foot Keekwulee Falls. There they noticed the ice field just above the falls.

"At first I thought, How cool—snow in August," says Corbett. "I assumed it was a patch about as big as a table, but I guess we were seeing it from far off."

As they hiked toward it, they realized they'd found more than a simple patch of melting snow.

They'd stumbled upon a yawning, crystalline cave carved and fluted by the waters of Denny Creek, spanning the entire mouth of the seventy-foot-wide canyon. Winter storms, blowing in off the Pacific, get snagged on the peaks of the Cascades and drop hundreds of inches of snow in the high country. An exceptionally wet winter had packed the narrow canyon above the falls with drifts. Wind, melting, and its own immense weight then compacted and compressed the snow into a white fang of ice hundreds of feet long and a dozen feet thick even in late August.

"It was beautiful," says Corbett—a jewel of winter glistening in the summer sun.

It was also deep, shadowy, cool against the heat of the hike— and enticing. Alec and Ollie posed while Corbett snapped a cell phone photo at the mouth of the cave, then the two boys turned and stepped inside.

"It was all echoey in there," Alec recalls. "There was steam rising off the snow, and it was hard to hear over the creek."

Moving deeper into the maze of ice and shadows, they saw a patch of light ahead, another way out.

"We had to cross a little channel of the creek," Alec says. "I used a stick to kind of pole-vault across, tossed it back to Ollie, and then turned around."

Behind him, Alec heard the crunch of his friend's shoes on the gravel. He saw Cyprus, his beagle, bolt from beneath his feet and scurry out of the cave. Seconds later, he heard a crash: "It was like snow falling off a roof but louder." Much louder.

A hundred feet away, YMCA camp counselor Tyson Goeppinger, who had led his own group up the mountain to see the ice cave minutes before, heard a deafening roar and felt the ground shake. He knew immediately what had happened.

"At first I thought how amazing it was to be near an ice cave when it collapsed," Goeppinger says. "But then I heard a woman screaming."

> Operator: Emergency. Fire and rescue.
>
> Joni Corbett: We are on a hike, the Lake Melakwa hike. My kids are in a snow cave, and it collapsed on them. Oh my God . . . They're suffocating. No!

Corbett's heart hammered in her chest, and her voice was shaking so much, she could hardly make herself understood.

> Operator: I need you to calm down so we can get you help.
>
> Corbett: We're going to need a helicopter or something. It collapsed, like, three minutes ago. Please hurry. Oh my God. Are you sending help? They are going to die.

Goeppinger ran toward the screams. Marilyn Pyke, leader of the church group just behind, arrived minutes later.

"We began crawling carefully around the ice, yelling the boys' names," she says. "The creek was moving under and around the ice. We put our heads down into any crack we could find and kept shouting their names, but there was no response."

All around them was a jumble of ice blocks shattered against rocks. Pyke and her group tried hacking at the blocks with sticks and shoving them with their legs, to no avail.

"At one point, I saw a block that had landed on a log about eighteen inches in diameter and just splintered it," Pyke says. "That's when I realized the tons of weight we were working against." There was nothing they could do but pull back, wait for help, and pray.

"I just kept thinking, They are going to come out," Gelmini recalls. "I thought they would walk out and be okay . . . any minute now." But the minutes passed; no one came out.

Under the ice, Alec was stunned but alive: "I didn't know what happened." A 40-by-50-foot section of the cave had collapsed on top of him, shoving him face-first into the ground. Only a small log directly ahead of him, about as big around as his waist, had kept him from being crushed. The log deflected some of the ice and created a small breathing space.

Still, his face was inches from the flowing creek, and the water was rising around the ice blocks that dammed its flow.

"Twice in the first couple of minutes, the water splashed me in the face and I'd have trouble breathing," he says. Both times, however, the ice shifted and the waters receded.

"I was pretty anxious. I tried to push myself up and break through, kind of doing push-ups to get it off my back, but it was too heavy." Exhausted, he laid his head on the log to quell his panic. "That's when I heard Ollie moaning."

His younger friend was pinned against a boulder nearby, his

left hand crushed under an ice block, his eyesight blurred by blood from cuts on his face.

"I couldn't see him, so I yelled to see if he was all right," Alec says. "But he just kept moaning."

Ollie had heard his friend, though. "The way I was pinned was making it really hard to breathe or talk, but I calmed down a little when I heard Alec's voice."

Alec shouted encouragement—"Hang on! Someone will be coming. Just hang on!"—and Ollie began calling back. In halting shouts edged with fear, they talked about their chances for rescue. They talked about Bishop Blanchet High School, where Alec would be a senior and Ollie a freshman, and anything they could think of, the sound of each other's voices a fragile lifeline between them. "Mostly we just kept telling each other to hold on," says Alec.

Wearing only sweatpants and ski jackets, trapped by ice and lying in water, the boys soon felt the cold. Alec knew they shouldn't fall asleep and kept asking Ollie if he was awake. But Alec was slipping into hypothermia himself.

"The way I was caught, my left leg was bent right up near my face, but I was so numb, I couldn't even feel my foot," he says. In the dark and barely able to move his hands, he leaned forward and bit down to see if it really was his foot. His tongue touched the sole of his boot. Thrashing around in an attempt to get free, he felt his right foot kick Ollie in the chest. "I hadn't realized he was so close. I reached out my hand as far as I could." Ollie reached out too. There, in the darkness, their fingers touched. Alec stopped struggling. The two boys held hands and waited.

Minutes after Joni Corbett's 911 call, an alarm crackled at the Eastside Fire and Rescue station in North Bend, ten miles from the Denny Creek trailhead. "A lot of the crew are hikers and skiers, so we knew the general area," says Cushman. "But there are a lot of steep gullies up there, a lot of slide areas, and we didn't know exactly what we'd end up getting into." They grabbed everything they thought they might need (shovels, pickaxes, a chain saw), drove to the trailhead, and hiked in.

What site commander Lt. Dean deAlteriis saw when he reached the creek an hour later made his heart sink.

"I didn't know what to expect with an ice collapse in August," he says, "but with victims under that much material for such a long time, I wasn't expecting a very good outcome. Still, you put those emotions aside and get to work."

First, they had to pick a spot to begin the excavation. There was a huge area—bigger than three fire engines, according to deAlteriis—to look for two boys. The searchers had one shot at getting it right.

After scrutinizing Corbett's cell phone photos of the boys, the rescuers first thought they should dig near the entrance. But Cushman had a different idea.

"I asked myself, *Where would I be?* And I had kind of a gut feeling—there's no other way to describe it. I just had a feeling where they would be."

He moved the operation forty feet upslope and said to the others, "Here. Let's dig right here." Although they wouldn't know it for hours yet, Cushman had marked a spot almost directly over Ollie Gelmini.

The boys were unaware of the frantic activity ten feet above them. "We couldn't hear anything. We just kept squeezing each other's hands to keep awake," Alec says. As two hours turned to three, their emotions leaped and tumbled.

"We'd convince each other that help was on its way, and then I'd think, I don't know how big this thing is. What if they can't find us?" When the sun came out above them, the cave would lighten, giving them hope. "Then it would dim and I'd think, *It's getting dark. The rescuers won't be able to get here*," says Alec.

Ollie counted the pebbles in the creek bed over and over; Alec watched the water drip—anything to keep their minds off dying. Then, in the silence, they heard a thud.

"It took a couple of whacks with the shovel to realize that this was an impossible task with hand tools," Cushman says. He yelled down to where the equipment was gathered, asking a crew member to bring him a chain saw.

"We brought the saw in the event that we would have to cut support timbers to shore up a collapse," says deAlteriis. "The idea of using it to cut the ice was a total surprise, but it worked great. Without that chain saw . . ." His voice trails off.

Even with the saw, and the two additional ones he radioed for, the task was painstaking: Cut a one-by-one-foot block, wrestle the slippery fifty-pound square out of the way and into the creek, cut another.

"We had to work carefully," deAlteriis says. "It was wet and slippery up there, and lifting the ice was very hard work."

They had to go slowly to make sure they didn't cut the boys.

Crews rotated out of the work site every twenty minutes to rest and warm up. One square foot at a time, they burrowed deeper into the heart of the cave and, they hoped, closer to the boys.

It was growing dark. A steady rain fell. Beneath a pine tree, curled in the fetal position, Joni Corbett was overcome.

"I just couldn't take it," she says, "the thought of the boys under there all that time."

She finally allowed herself to be led down the mountain with the girls to a medic site set up at the trailhead while Chrissy Gelmini stayed near the cave.

"They couldn't have dragged me off that mountain," Gelmini says.

But she, too, felt hope fading.

"There was a point," she says, "when I thought, I have to release my son. I thought he was dead, and I had to come to grips with that."

Then she heard someone shout, "They've heard a voice!"

Cushman was jammed way down in a crack in the ice almost at creek level, still shouting and listening, shouting and listening, when he thought he heard a low moan. He yelled back over his shoulder, "Everybody, quiet!"

The saws were shut down. Radios ceased crackling. The whole mountain seemed to go silent. Then he heard the sound again.

"We've got someone alive down here!" Cushman shouted. Then they heard a second voice. The chain saws snapped back to life. Ice flew out of the hole.

"When we heard the voices, everything changed," deAlteriis says. "But we had to be careful. There was still a lot of ice to move."

As they dug closer to the voices, only a few feet from the spot where Cushman had told them to work, they switched to pickaxes and shovels.

"We got to Ollie first," Cushman says. "We almost had him free, but the block pinning his hand was just too big. 'I have to run a chain saw above you,' I told him. He got pretty nervous, but our time was getting short."

Five hours after the cave had collapsed, Ollie Gelmini was lifted from the ice. Medics secured him to a backboard, gave him an IV to prevent dehydration, and applied warming packets to raise his body temperature. On the narrow path, rescuers passed him hand to hand out to where his mother was waiting. His face was covered with blood and his eyes were closed, but when he heard his mother's voice, "he looked at me and I knew it was Ollie," Gelmini says.

Waiting at the medic station down the mountain, Joni Corbett knew only what was relayed by radio.

"I knew they had gotten one of the boys out, but the rescuers couldn't or wouldn't tell me which one," she says. "Then I heard someone say that the boy still in the ice was really worked up and wanted to get out now." She thought that might be Alec.

"Once Ollie was out, that's when I got the most anxious. Then I was alone," Alec says. "I was having a hard time breathing. I wanted the ice off my back. I remember they were whacking it with ice axes. I wanted them to stop, but they said no. So I just shut my mouth and waited."

The one huge chunk of ice still pinning him was teetering dangerously just above his back. If it fell the wrong way, it would crush him, but it was too risky to use the saw this close. While one rescuer struggled to hold the block in place, others tried to crack it with ice picks, blow upon blow, each one sending a shot of pain through Alec's back.

Finally, the block broke. Thirty minutes after Ollie was taken out of the ice and five and a half hours after the collapse, both boys were free. As rescuers pulled Alec out, he looked down at the log he'd been pinned near.

"My first thought was, If I'd taken one more step, I'd be dead."

His second thought was about Cyprus: "Has anyone seen a beagle?"

Both dogs were safe, at the medic station, but the danger wasn't over.

"All the while, I'd been watching a crack in the second part of the ice cave," Cushman says. "When we started, it was about the size of my fist. By the time we got Alec out and down to the helicopter, it was more than two feet across."

Eight minutes after rescue personnel cleared the area, that part of the cave gave way, burying the spot where the boys had been trapped and the rescuers had worked.

A helicopter airlifted Ollie and Alec to Seattle's Harborview Medical Center, where doctors found that both boys had broken backs. Ollie had nerve damage in his left hand and lacerations on his face. Alec's left foot was broken. Both suffered from hypothermia and dehydration, and both needed surgery and months of physical therapy. But they're expected to fully recover.

"There must be a greater plan for those two," deAlteriis says. "They certainly got a second chance."

Three days after the rescue, Brian Corbett, Alec's father, who had first introduced his family to the Denny Creek Trail, sat in a chair next to Alec's bed with his hand on his sleeping son's shoulder.

"Around 3 a.m., Alec woke up and started describing a nightmare to me," his father says. "In the dream, he was still in the ice, and the rescuers weren't coming."

Still in pain and heavily medicated, Alec told the story calmly and quietly as his father choked back tears.

"He finished telling me and went right back to sleep like it was no big deal," Corbett says. Then, next to Alec's bed, he wept.

AT THE MERCY OF A WILD ANIMAL

SWARM!

BY GERRY JOHNSON

Debbie Jacoby Walker lifted her gaze and smiled. Above the century-old cypress and water oaks of the Florida marsh, eagles glided across the afternoon sky. Here and there she caught sight of blue herons standing silently and still.

Having grown up in Maryland, the 41-year-old mother of two still felt a certain trepidation entering this wild jungle terrain. The steamy realm of alligators and water moccasins was not her element. But high atop her husband Ben's home-built swamp buggy—a tanklike, open-air machine with six-foot-tall tractor tires—she felt safe.

That late October day in 1995 was the start of hunting season, and 46-year-old Ben had left his nursery business in Naples, Florida, to scout for deer and wild boar. The native Floridian had brought Debbie and their boys, Matthew, four, and Mark, two, along.

Tired from their long day and lulled by the machine's rocking, the boys were now napping in back. Beneath their elevated seats, Ben's two hunting dogs lay quietly in a large cage.

"Shouldn't we head back?" Debbie asked.

"All we've got to do is follow our own tracks, and we'll be back before sunset," Ben assured her.

The swamp buggy became entangled in branches, and Ben climbed onto one of the huge tires to cut them away. A moment later, above the rumble of the idling engine, Debbie heard a high-pitched yelp from the dogs. Then Ben cried out, "Oh, my God."

"What's wrong?" she asked. Ben was clawing at his jeans. Debbie looked down and saw, from Ben's ankles to his thighs, a blanket of vibrating, probing yellow jackets.

Within seconds, thousands of wasps had engulfed the swamp buggy in a cloud of fury. Debbie felt the stiletto jab of scores of tiny stingers.

The boys! She turned to see wasps swarming over her sleeping children. Matthew awoke screaming, helplessly waving his arms. She heard two-year-old Mark cry, "Mommy, make it stop!"

Fighting his way back into his seat, Ben jammed the transmission into reverse, but the gears would not engage. "We have to run," he yelled. "I'll go first. Throw the babies down to me."

Ben leapt blindly into the tall subtropic grass. His right leg landed on something rock-hard and buckled beneath him. A searing pain shot through his body.

"Debbie, wait!" He dragged himself to the rear of the vehicle. "Drop Mark here! The ground's soft."

Debbie hesitated. How could she toss her baby almost 12 feet down? Then the great angry swirl slammed into her from behind. Debbie screamed and dropped Mark as she doubled over in agony.

The boy landed in the mud unhurt, and Ben dragged him away from the buggy. Debbie dropped Matthew, then tumbled down after him.

Still locked in their cage, the dogs howled forlornly. Debbie's heart broke. *I can't help them now,* she thought. *I've got to think of my family.* She pulled Matthew away from the buggy.

"We've got to shield the kids," she shouted. She and Ben began brushing the wasps off them and rolling the boys in the mud. But everything seemed vague and hazy. *I've lost my glasses!* Debbie realized. Extremely nearsighted, she needed glasses even to find her way around the house.

Ben glanced at Debbie. Yellow jackets covered her face like a writhing mask. Already her cheeks, forehead and chin were starting to swell—sign of an allergic reaction that could send her into fatal shock.

"Take Mark and move back down the trail, Deb," Ben ordered. "I'll send Matt after you."

Picking up the boy, Debbie stumbled along the buggy tracks as far as she could from the yellow jackets. The swarm finally stopped pursuing her.

"Follow Mom," Ben told Matthew hoarsely. "She'll take care of you."

The frightened four-year-old, still covered with yellow jackets, crawled away. When Debbie saw him coming alone, she realized Ben must be too injured to walk. "Stay here," she told the kids. Head down, arms flailing, she re-entered the yellow storm.

"Try to walk, Ben—I'll help you," she said between gasping breaths. But Debbie couldn't lift the six-foot-one-inch, 220-pound man. "Oh, Ben," she cried, "what are we going to do?" Her speech was beginning to slur.

Ben knew they were in trouble. He was in terrible pain, and Debbie was going into shock—she had been stung before, and reacted to it so badly that she'd had to seek hospital treatment. No one knew where they were, and night was coming on.

"Listen to me, Deb," he said. "You've got to run for help. Leave the babies."

"I can't!" she said.

"They'll slow you down. Go while you still can. Follow the buggy tracks back to the camp we passed."

Seeing her incapacitated husband and hearing her two small boys sobbing, Debbie knew she had no choice. "I love you, Ben. I'll try my best."

Ben watched her stumble out of sight. It seemed impossible she would make it in her condition. But the couple shared a deep Christian faith. He began to pray, asking for just one special person to help his family.

Debbie staggered through the muck, trying desperately to keep between the huge tire tracks. Without her glasses, everything was a blur. Her mind was dull, her body lethargic.

The insect venom was doing its heinous, silent work. As anaphylactic shock sets in, the venom allergens first lower blood pressure, reducing oxygen flow to the brain, heart and other vital organs. Then external body tissues, also shortchanged of oxygen, open their cellular doors to fluids. These tissues swell, closing the throat and air passages. Some victims die quickly; others suffocate slowly.

Debbie was entering the early stages. And without knowing it, she had wandered off the buggy track.

Phil Pelletier had been looking forward to this hunting trip with his buddies for a long time. Yet the morning's hunt had been disappointing for the 45-year-old county recreation director. There had been plenty of game and his friends were in a festive mood, but something was tugging at him. He elected to stay behind to pack up their camp. He wasn't sure why.

It was 4:25 p.m. before he headed his truck down the narrow, abandoned railroad bed they used for a road. Within a hundred yards, a figure appeared. It was a woman, staggering and covered with mud, her face grotesquely swollen. *Lord*, he thought, *she's been beaten up bad!*

"Lady, are you all right?"

At the sound of his gentle voice, Debbie began screaming. "My babies are dead! My husband broke his leg . . . attacked by yellow jackets. They were all over us!"

"I'll help you," Pelletier said, trying to calm her. "We'll go look for them."

"I can't," she gasped. "My throat is closing. I need medicine." There was an unnatural look in her eyes, and her skin was a lifeless pale gray.

"I'll take you to Ortona," Pelletier said. "It's five minutes away. There's a store there. We can call for help."

Paramedics met them there and quickly gave Debbie an epinephrine injection. Her condition was listed as priority one: life-threatening.

As the paramedics worked, Debbie did not take her eyes off

Pelletier, pleading with him to go back and look for her family. A father of two, he could only imagine her anguish.

"Don't worry," he told the half-conscious mother. "I'll find your family."

Sweat trickled down Pelletier's back as he pushed his pickup to nearly 60 m.p.h. along the railroad bed into the swamp. Debbie had described to him the place where she came out of the woods. Suddenly Pelletier noticed an opening and slammed on the brakes. *Maybe this is the spot,* he thought.

But the pickup dipped low into the mushy, swollen marsh and began sinking. Quickly he backed up onto the railroad bed and drove on.

Fifty feet later, he found another narrow gap. He recalled there were old logging roads snaking through these woods. *That must be the way she walked out.*

Daylight was fading. Pelletier pushed ahead without any sign of a trail. The staccato of fan blades hitting water kept him apprised of how deep his truck had sunk in the soggy terrain. A half-mile passed before a flash of color caught his eye.

He idled the truck and looked again. There, sitting in a shallow water hole, was a little boy! He was facing away, talking to himself. Not wanting to alarm him, Pelletier called from a distance, "I've got your mama!"

At the sound of a voice, the child turned and started to cry. Pelletier was un-prepared for the sight. Four-year-old Matthew's neck, arms and legs had swelled to grotesque proportions. His ears stuck straight out from his head. His skin—stretched tight and bloodlessly white—revealed hundreds of crimson-purple bites.

Scooping up the boy, Pelletier gently carried him to the truck. Matthew screamed and wriggled in pain. He began to shake, cold even in the ninety degree weather. Staring blankly, he put his head down. *He's slipping away from me,* thought Pelletier. He had to get the child to a hospital. This was one life he could save.

Heading out, Pelletier tried to avoid water holes. By the third one, his luck ran out. As water covered the pickup's hood, its engine stalled. Picking up Matthew, now limp, Pelletier waded into the hip-deep pond.

Then, across a clearing, he spotted a man. It was Deputy Sheriff Carlin Coleman, who had followed Pelletier's tracks to the spot.

"This boy needs help!" Pelletier called. "The only way we're going to bring the others out is with a swamp buggy." He told Coleman about a friend's buggy at his camp.

The two men had driven only a short distance when they met Fire Chief Dennis Hollingsworth. The three decided Coleman would take the boy on to the store at Ortona, while Pelletier and Hollingsworth went back to the swamp in the borrowed buggy. It was 6:37 p.m. In an hour, their chances of finding Mark and Ben Walker would be virtually nil.

Back on the trail, Hollingsworth noticed a section of rutted mud. "Hold it," he commanded. "There are two sets of buggy tracks, one big, one small. They cross right here."

"The woman told me her husband has a big buggy," Pelletier said. "If she got mixed up here and followed the small tracks, it would account for her getting to my camp so fast. It was the luckiest thing she could have done."

The two men followed the big ruts to a pond surrounded by thick palmetto grasses. Looking across, Pelletier caught the outline of a head.

Jumping into the pond, Hollingsworth furiously waded through the murky waters. There he saw the bloated, ashen face of Mark Walker. The fire chief choked back tears as he cradled the muddy toddler in his arms. "We'll get you out of here, little buddy," he promised.

He radioed his dispatcher. "We've got him," he said, his voice breaking. "We'll bring him out, then go back in for his daddy." It was agreed that Coleman would come and take the child to the Ortona store.

Ben Walker hadn't moved since Debbie left. He had called to his boys and got no answer, so he feared they had wandered off after their mother and were hopelessly lost. His only relief was that the yellow jackets had lost interest in him. They had targeted the swamp buggy, its engine still rumbling, as their enemy.

Ben was in great pain, drifting toward unconsciousness, when he heard the sound of another buggy. A man's voice rang out: "Ben? You all right? We're coming, Ben."

"Thank you, God," Ben cried. "Thank you."

Shortly after, hunters went in to retrieve Ben's swamp buggy—and to free his dogs, who survived. The vehicle was moved, but wasps returned to it, even after being burned off. Finally, hunters burned the nest. Most yellow-jacket nests lie beneath the earth, but this one had expanded above ground to include a fallen tree. The nest was apparently disrupted when the Walkers' swamp buggy hit it with a tire.

At Columbia East Pointe Hospital, Debbie was brought back from the edge of death. Compound fractures in Ben's right knee and upper leg required several operations, but he is now back at work. The boys recovered quickly, and no longer have bad dreams. Replacing the family's memories of terror and pain is a heightened awareness of love, an emotion that moves people to acts of spontaneous courage and sacrifice.

Around the Ortona store they still talk about the inexplicable connections—the timely appearances of the right people at the right time; how every seemingly wrong turn ended up being right. They call it a miracle.

SHARK ATTACK—ON LAND

BY ANDREA COOPER

Chuck Anderson breathed deeply as he stepped into choppy waters along the Gulf Shores public beach in Alabama. The day was hazy but pretty, only 6:30 a.m. and already warm. Several times a week, the 44-year-old assistant principal and former football coach at Robertsdale High School in Robertsdale, Alabama, trained with friends for triathlons. They swam, ran and cycled, sometimes all in a single day. The plan today was to swim a mile and bike for 40. Anderson's body, at six feet and 230 pounds, was powerful. In his weight category, he had won more than 30 triathlons—and wanted more.

After seven years of triathlon training and countless swims in the Gulf of Mexico, Anderson still felt apprehensive when entering the water. It wasn't the temperature, brisk but refreshing for June. It wasn't the stingrays, though he once stepped on one at this beach and remembered the feeling of poison seeping through his system as he drove himself to the hospital. It was the sharks.

Years ago Anderson had spent a summer running a chartered dive boat in the Florida Keys. He had looked a few sharks in the eye—and teeth—through his diving mask. He liked to think he had the caution that comes from familiarity.

Sharks were common in the Gulf, and sometimes Anderson and his buddies grabbed one another's ankles in the water to see who might shriek. But no unprovoked attacks had been recorded on an Alabama beach. That morning Anderson met two of his training partners, Karen Forfar, 63, and Richard Watley, 55, on the beach, and they plunged into the water together. As usual, Watley swam out toward some buoys—too far from land for Anderson's taste. But Watley always did things his own way.

Theirs was an unusual friendship. At a competition in the early 1990s, a stranger sprinted up alongside Anderson and ragged him: "Fat Boy, you're not going to beat me." After the race, Watley walked over to his opponent, put out his hand and introduced himself. They decided to train together—the assistant principal with the master's degree, and the barber whose past included a tour as a demolition specialist in Vietnam. They gave each other nicknames. Anderson was the Big Dummy. Watley was Buckethead.

Karen Forfar and Anderson swam past the Pink Pony Pub, whose pier had been knocked down by a hurricane. Its pilings were a submerged hazard. When he reached the spot, he stopped to warn Forfar so she'd be sure to avoid them. He glanced at his watch: 6:38 a.m. There was a strong wind kicking up a little chop, but they were making good time. Then he bumped into something.

It jostled his hips, half-rolling him. He had a strange feeling that it wasn't a piling.

It was a shark.

He righted himself, treading in ten feet of water, and yelled to Karen, "Shark! Shark! Get out!" Forfar immediately struck out for shore. Anderson stuck his face in the water, open-eyed. The shark was two feet away and headed straight toward him. God, its head was enormous, wider than any he'd seen. Its eyes were dark and cold, almost hollow. A wave of terror roiled inside him.

"No! Stop! Stop!" he screamed, as if hollering at a dog. Anderson had encountered big dogs on his runs and always scared them off. But a shark wouldn't be deterred by noise. Instinctively he back paddled, sticking out his arms, palms forward. The shark snapped. It sheared four fingers off his right hand. Blood gushed out, staining the water.

Then his athletic training clicked in. As a coach, he taught players to tune out distractions. The marching band could be playing, people cheering or booing, but he showed them how to focus. He seized on the thought: *I am going to live.*

Waves bobbing to his face, Anderson treaded water toward shore. The shark circled, following him—a gray living submarine taking direct aim. It lunged and grazed past his belly. *I'm not sure it got me that time,* he thought. But it had, gouging a wound two inches wide.

Anderson was barely moving toward shore. Blood gushed from his hand. I'm not going fast enough to get away, he realized. The shark charged again. Anderson held out his arms to ward off the attack, but the shark grabbed his right forearm and flipped over and dived. It dragged him to the bottom, scraping his knees against the sand. He struggled desperately, banging his left hand against the shark's impenetrable skin. The shark rolled, head thrashing side to side. It was trying to take off Anderson's right arm.

Finally it swam to the surface, giving him a chance to take gulps of air. Then it dived again, and dragged his feet along the Gulf floor. Suddenly they were in knee-deep water—on a sand bar.

Anderson struggled to regain his footing, his arm still clenched in the shark's mouth. A third of the shark's body sprawled across the sand. It was at least seven feet long. He saw its teeth for the first time. Razor-sharp, serrated, tearing at his arm.

Anderson snapped. He felt an animal rage. "Damn it. You're not going to take me away from my children!" he screamed. He worked his arm up and down, trying to pull free. Sharks are virtually silent, but then Anderson heard an eerie sound. Something popped. The force propelled him backward onto the sand bar. His right forearm was still in the shark's mouth. Its eyes rolled back. Then he couldn't take in any more of the unspeakable sight.

He felt bone, a phantom tingling, and staggered to the shore holding his arm upright, out of his line of vision—afraid he'd faint if he saw it. Forfar was right behind him and rushed to help. Anderson was screaming, "Watley! Get out of the water!"

Richard Watley heard a distant shout but didn't look up at first, assuming Anderson had encountered jellyfish. They could burn, but weren't serious. When he checked the beach some

100 feet away, he saw his friend bent over, clutching his arm.

At five feet, eight inches and 180 pounds, Watley didn't consider himself a natural swimmer, but he was tough. Anderson once described him as a guy so cool-headed he could smile at an attacking dog.

Swimming in, Watley's knee hit something solid yet spongy. Probably a log, he thought, and tried to resume swimming. But suddenly he came to a dead stop and found himself stretched out on the water. *What in the hell?* he thought. He wondered if he'd run aground.

Something was under him. He saw the head. The black eyes. Open mouth. A shark. That's what got Chuck, he realized. And now it wanted him.

Watley gasped, dodging the shark, somehow managing to push it away. He heard himself hyperventilating. His mind fixed on one idea: *Man, you better get it together, or you're dead.*

His shove put about five feet between them. Watley didn't scream, didn't talk, just concentrated on what he had to do. As the shark surged forward, Watley grabbed its snout and hung on, using all his strength to keep the jaws away. The shark thrashed, apparently surprised. Watley balled his fist and punched the shark's snout. It felt like the hard plastic of a steering wheel. His hand throbbed.

He glanced up toward land, gauging the distance—a third of a football field. A strange calm settled on him. *I've got too far to go,* he thought. *I'm going to die. But I'm not going without a fight.* In Vietnam, he had experienced a feeling of controlled fright. There was afraid, and there was smart afraid. He would be smart afraid.

Watley made for shore, watching a dark shadow circle counterclockwise through the water underneath him. When the shark surfaced, Watley lunged forward, grabbing its head. He held on as it shook him violently back and forth, up and down, on the surface, then underwater. He felt its teeth pierce his thigh, leaving a grisly four-inch gash, distinct as the slice of a knife.

Then it released him and began to circle. When it struck, he clutched its snout with his left hand and pushed with his right. It pulled away again, giving him a few seconds to swim toward land. Watley swam a six-second burst, and then looked back. No sign of the shark.

Suddenly, out of nowhere, it charged at tremendous speed. Desperately, Watley gripped its head. The shark reared, lifting him out of the water. He grabbed its fin and threw his weight on the beast, slowing it. Its gill slits were exposed and Watley punched them, giving it everything he had. The shark simply flapped its fins and broke free.

Once more, Watley started for shore and the shark followed him. But its next attack wasn't as fierce. Had it had enough? Then Watley touched sand. The shark had pushed him closer to the beach. He was in chest-deep water. As a wave plunged over them, he clamped one hand on the shark and took the beast to the bottom, punching with his other, the blows slowed by the water. Surprisingly, the shark retreated. And a wave pushed Watley toward the shore.

When he reached the beach, he saw people gathered on the boardwalk—Anderson among them. He felt a burst of joy and exhilaration.

Nine days after the attack, Chuck Anderson celebrated Father's Day in the hospital with his parents and children. In all, he underwent nine operations and skin grafts to save his elbow. Watley had no serious injury.

The two resumed training as soon as possible, though it took Anderson a while to get used to the water. Not out of undue fear—he just had to change his stroke because of his new prosthesis. In April 2001 he entered his first triathlon since the attack, and won his division.

CORNERED

BY KENNETH MILLER

Nothing about the River Trail suggests it might be a place where death waits patiently in the shadows. The footpath, in Central California's Sequoia National Forest, winds above the swift Kern River, passing through stands of incense cedar, live oak and digger pine. The grade is gentle, a state highway runs close by, and the laughter of kayakers floats up from the glittering stream. Families often crowd the trail, heading for a swim or an hour or two of fishing.

On June 26, 2004, a young medical-equipment saleswoman named Shannon Parker set off down the path, dressed in tennis shoes, a tank top and a bikini bottom. Her boyfriend of 18 months, Loyola University law student Mathias Maciejewski, and his classmates Jason Quirino and Ben Marsh were with her. It was six o'clock on a Saturday evening, and though the summer sun was still far from setting, the narrow canyon was already growing dark. The four friends were the only hikers. But they were not alone.

Despite the scenery, Shannon, 27, didn't much want to be there. A proudly citified country girl, she saw little point in hiking; for exercise, she preferred the health club near her apartment in Santa Monica, more than 100 miles due south. Her idea of beauty had more to do with firm abs, a good hairdo and a sexy pair of jeans than with an untamed landscape. When she went to the beach, she kept to the sand—the thought of sharks made her nervous. Mathias, however, was an avid trekker who'd bagged peaks in Ecuador and Peru. He begged her to join his weekend expedition, so she drove in from her parents' place in nearby Bakersfield. The group spent the day playing in the river, and planned to have a last splash before returning to camp for dinner.

After they walked about a mile, Mathias declared that he had found the perfect spot. To Shannon, however, the path down to the water appeared treacherous; she'd had enough boulder-hopping for one day. "I'm going to the car," she called as the guys sprinted for the rapids.

"I dropped my sunglasses somewhere," Mathias hollered back. "See if you can find them." Shannon hadn't gone far when she found something else: a dun-colored mountain lion, crouching 20 feet in front of her in the brush along the edge of the trail. She and the animal locked eyes for a split second. Then it hissed, bared its teeth and leapt.

According to researchers, there've been just 88 mountain lion attacks in North America since 1890, and 20 were fatal. Dogs kill about a dozen people every year—"way more than have been killed by cougars," says Lynn Sadler, president of the

Mountain Lion Foundation, a conservation group based in Sacramento, California. The predators' main quarry is deer, and no one knows why they occasionally sample human flesh. One theory is mistaken identity: A cougar's eyesight relies largely on shape and movement, and under certain circumstances a person may resemble meatier prey.

However rare, there is a special, primal horror in a cougar attack—one that calls up some of our species' most ancient nightmares. A mountain lion generally kills a deer by crushing the animal's windpipe in its powerful jaws. Since humans have shorter necks, cougars most often latch onto the head, and then shake the victim back and forth like a house cat playing with a bird.

That's what happened to Shannon. The cougar clamped its sharp teeth onto the right side of her face and pulled her to the ground. But she fought back. She pummeled and kicked. She thrust her hand into the lion's mouth to keep its jaws from closing tighter. At 5'3", she was smaller than her 6' adversary, but her gym-toned muscles served her well. So did her attitude. "She was always super-stubborn," says her younger brother, Raymond. "She was beautiful, she was sweet, but she wasn't gonna roll over for anyone."

As they struggled, the combatants slid down the steep embankment; they came to rest about 20 feet off the trail, with Shannon on her knees, her head to the ground, the lion still locked on. Her body lay roughly parallel with the river, 80 feet below. The cougar tried to drag her farther into the brush, but she held fast, bracing her feet against a boulder and a tree. The two fell into a stalemate, the silence broken only by the crea-

ture's panting. Shannon felt no pain—her adrenaline and en-
dorphins took care of that—and she was more furious than
afraid. This is ridiculous, she thought. I'm not going to die. She
spent a moment praying before she began to scream Mathias's
name.

Mathias and Shannon were a striking couple; his dark, chis-
eled features nicely complemented her pert good looks. They
were equally obstinate as well, though he tended to be taciturn,
while she could be impatient and volatile. They had locked
horns often, over everything from where to have dinner to
where their relationship was heading. Back at the swimming
spot, Mathias decided that it would be better to catch up with
Shannon, so the guys ditched their plan to take another plunge
in the river. A few minutes after she left, Mathias climbed back
up to the trail, with Jason and Ben straggling behind. Then
he heard her. "I could tell she was hurt by the way she was
screaming," he says. "I thought she'd fallen off the trail and
hurt herself."

He broke into a run, and as he drew closer he saw that something had her by the head. Mathias, who grew up in Hawaii,
had never seen a cougar; at first he took it for a badger. He
yelled to his friends to hurry, and skidded down the ravine. Not
until he reached Shannon did he realize what she was grap-
pling with. The beast stared at him impassively, its eyes golden
and unfathomable. It smelled slightly gamy. "Please get it off
me," Shannon cried.

"I will, babe," he answered, and she immediately grew calmer.
Mathias is a methodical man, given to quick decisions and

the relentless pursuit of their conclusions. This situation, how-ever, was unlike anything he had encountered on South American peaks or in his two years of law school. His first thought was to simply pull Shannon away; he hoped that the lion would lunge at him and let her go, and that he could then somehow kick it down the hill. He positioned himself behind her and wrapped his arms around her waist. But as he tugged, the cougar pulled in the opposite direction, its teeth piercing deeper into her face. "No, no, no," Shannon said. "That hurts."

By then, the others had arrived. Jason tossed Ben his truck keys and shouted, "Go get help!" As Ben ran toward the trail-head, Jason and Mathias tried to frighten the lion off, shaking their fists and shouting obscenities.

Then Mathias remembered Jason's hunting knife; the guys had teased him about it earlier that day, saying, "What are you planning to use that for, dude?" Standing over the squatting Mathias, Jason passed his friend the weapon. Mathias plunged the three-inch blade into the animal's shoulder, but there was no reaction. He pulled it out and tried again, jabbing desper-ately; somehow, the knife slipped from his hand and tumbled into the ravine. The cougar made a low growl, but it didn't budge.

Jason tried kicking the lion, but lost his footing on the steep incline. "Rocks! Hit it with rocks!" Mathias yelled. Jason, who stands 6'2", hurled a football-sized stone at the cougar's back, to no avail. He tried again: nothing. But with the fourth blow, the lion released its grip and stumbled away. Jason grabbed Shan-non's arms, and Mathias began pushing her up the hill.

Before they could reach the top, the cougar sprang forward

and fastened onto Shannon's right leg with its teeth and claws. "Smash its head!" Mathias cried. Until then, Jason had avoided the animal's most vulnerable part, because Shannon's head might have been injured as well. But now he had a clear shot, and he began slamming the lion's skull with all his strength. Under normal conditions, Jason is a gentle, thoughtful man; before studying law, he had earned a master's in history. "I'd been in fights when I was younger," he says, "but I'd never felt that wild or uncontrollable. I felt all the hatred I'd ever felt in my life." At last the thick bone cracked, and the cougar went staggering down the hill.

Mathias and Jason hauled Shannon back up to the trail, and were stunned by the extent of her injuries. She was covered with blood, dirt and the cougar's saliva, and the right side of her body was raked with claw marks and abrasions. During the nine-minute struggle, half her nose had been ripped away. Her right eye had been crushed, its upper and lower lids peeled off, and there was a hole where the left eye's tear duct had been. Her top lip was torn in two; a line of puncture wounds marched up her cheek. A chunk of her thigh was also missing, exposing bare muscle and bone.

Still, when her friends asked her if she could walk, she said, "Let's go!" As Mathias helped her hobble toward the trailhead, Jason walked backward, carrying a big stone and watching for the enemy. It took 40 minutes to reach the parking lot, where Ben was waiting with a ranger; it would be another 45 minutes before an ambulance arrived. The guys laid Shannon down, placed a towel under her head, and tried to make her comfortable, but the shock of what had happened to her finally set in.

Trembling and weeping, she asked over and over again: "Am I going to die?"

She did not die. That was the cougar's fate, after Jason and Ben led wildlife officers to the place where it still stood, dazed and wobbling. It took a couple of shots to kill the cat, which proved to be only two years old and severely emaciated; experts guessed that a wildfire had forced it from its usual hunting grounds, and that stronger males had run it off their territory. At 58 pounds, it weighed half as much as a normal cougar, and 50 pounds less than Shannon herself. Its attack—and its uncanny persistence—was evidently prompted by sheer starvation.

Shannon's suffering was of a different kind. A helicopter met the ambulance at Kernville Airport, and flew her to Kern Medical Center in Bakersfield. Mathias had phoned her parents—Randy, a bankruptcy trustee, and Kay, a homemaker—and when they arrived, the doctors told them that they must not cry in front of their daughter. Shannon tried to comfort them, murmuring, "It's going to be okay, Mom," through her tattered lips. After she was stabilized, another copter ferried her to UCLA Medical Center in Los Angeles. Randy and Kay followed in the car, with Mathias as their passenger on the grim two-hour journey. As they traveled, surgeons were assembling to handle the complex case.

At six o'clock Sunday morning, Shannon went into the operating room. A general surgeon attended to her limbs and torso, an ocular surgeon worked on her eyes, and a plastic surgeon—Dr. Robert Schwarcz, who would shepherd her through many more procedures—made initial repairs to her face. Schwarcz found what appeared to be a piece of the cougar's tooth lodged in the left side of her nasal bone. He had operated on victims of pit bulls trained to tear human flesh, but this mauling was the worst he'd ever seen.

When the patient emerged at one o'clock that afternoon, her family hardly recognized her. "Her face was so swollen, you can't even imagine," says Kay. "There was not one place on her body that didn't look like it had been torn apart." Such injuries would be traumatic for anyone, physically and emotionally, but they were doubly devastating for a young woman whose sense of self was tied closely to her beauty. "Growing up, she thought she had to look perfect," her mother recalls.

Shannon had struggled with an eating disorder as a weight-obsessed teenager; as an adult, one of her favorite pastimes was clothes shopping. "It was important to me to really spend some time each morning getting ready—makeup, all that stuff," Shannon says. "I put a lot into looking good."

Now her routine would be very different. That Tuesday, when Shannon had recovered sufficiently from the surgery, Kay combed the twigs and tangles out of her daughter's hair and washed it a dozen times. Then grooming took a backseat to wound care. Mathias and Shannon's family sat by her bedside and on doctors' orders took turns around the clock slathering her skin with neomycin. She proved to be allergic to the antibiotic salve, and the blistering rash added to her agony. Meanwhile, scoop-hungry reporters were trying to sneak past hospital security. Shannon couldn't face them; she couldn't even face herself.

On Wednesday, she caught a glimpse of her reflection and

dissolved in sobs. "I was just crushed," she says. One moment, she would be joking with her family and friends; the next, she would be seized with gloom or panic. On Friday, when it was time to leave the medical center, Shannon needed a sedative just to make it to the car.

She settled in with her parents at the Bakersfield farmhouse where her mother had grown up. Her brother covered all the mirrors, but no one could protect her from the phantoms that stalked her mind. In the beginning, she slept on the floor by her parents' bed. When the night terrors came, her mother would join her on one side of the mattress; the family dachshund, Rudy, would settle on the other. During the day, the slightest surprise would touch off fits of weeping, especially when someone approached her from her blind right side. "I didn't mean to make a big deal out of it," she says, "but the mountain lion had come up out of nowhere, and anything that startled me sent me back to that situation."

To avoid such shocks, Kay installed a bell (the kind used at hotel reception desks) down the hall from Shannon's bedroom; all visitors were required to ring it. After every crisis, her mother would remind Shannon of her blessings: "We would sit and talk about how lucky we are, because we can see, and we are alive, and we have a great family," says Kay. "And we're going to get better."

Gradually, with the help of a therapist, Shannon's moods stabilized. But her anguish has not been only emotional. After three futile attempts to reattach her cornea, her right eye was removed last February—in part to ward off a condition known as sympathetic ophthalmia, which sometimes attacks the good eye of a person whose other one has stopped functioning. Shannon now wears a silicon-and-acrylic prosthesis, tethered to her eye muscles so that it moves naturally. She also wears glasses to protect her left eye from accidents. She has learned to drive with impaired depth perception, but handshakes remain a baffling visual challenge.

Over the past year and a half, she has endured a total of six major surgeries. Last August, Dr. Schwarcz and a partner, Dr. Ronald Strahan, rebuilt her nose. They shored up the left nostril and reopened the airway, which had been blocked by displaced cartilage. Dr. Schwarcz also evened out her lip line, using fat liposuctioned from her abdomen. Just after Christmas, he performed an eyelid lift on her right eye, to eliminate a pronounced droop, and created a pouch of skin to replace her ruined left tear duct. Schwarcz worked on her lips again as well, using another dose of belly fat to improve their symmetry. She will need at least two more operations before the reconstruction process is complete.

After each surgery, Schwarcz injects an excruciating cocktail of steroids and chemotherapy agents into the incisions, to help speed healing and minimize scarring. Some scars are inevitable, though, and during most operations Schwarcz performs an additional procedure to correct marks left by the earlier surgeries. Scar revision, as it is called, involves making a series of incisions across the offending tissue. "You cut out the parts that are sunken or raised and try to make it flat," Schwarcz explains. "I do it in the shape of a W, which breaks up the scar and makes it look less linear."

The discomfort caused by all these procedures is difficult

to comprehend; each surgery requires weeks of recovery time. Shannon shrugs off the misery. "It doesn't bother me anymore," she says with a laugh. "They can stick me anywhere, and I'm completely immune to it." In truth, her stoicism comes from a fierce mental discipline. "From early on, I had a strong trust in my surgeon. I knew everything he did to me was to help me. And with that, I was willing to take anything. I just made myself numb."

The rewards are finally coming. Last October, she returned to her job selling medical equipment; in December, she moved to a new apartment in Santa Monica. She credits her doctors and loved ones for speeding her climb back to independence, including friends and relatives who pitched in to help pay the $26,000 in ambulance and helicopter bills not covered by insurance.

Mathias, sadly, no longer figures in her support network; their relationship ended three months after the attack, strained to breaking by the travails that followed. Still, Shannon supported his selection last summer, along with Jason (with whom she keeps in touch), for a Carnegie Medal for heroism. "I've thanked Mathias a million times," she says. "I wouldn't be here without him."

Those who know Shannon speak of her as a hero as well. They marvel at her fighting spirit, and at her refusal to complain about her long tribulation. "She keeps her eye on the goal as opposed to her pain, which is amazing," says Schwarcz, who notes that many patients with lesser problems surrender to rage or despair.

Shannon's appearance has been restored to the point where, once again, the first impression she makes is "pretty girl." She's back at the gym, and she occasionally visits the local nightspots for drinks with friends. But her ordeal has reordered her values. "Before the accident, I was kind of wrapped up in myself," she says. "I didn't really read much. I worked a lot. I liked to go out and have a good time. I was never too interested in art or theater or traveling to other countries. Now I am." She's less preoccupied with mirrors. And she's far more eager to help others in need, whether by tending to an ailing aunt or giving motivational speeches to Bakersfield women's groups. "I get up and tell my story; I encourage them not to obsess over the small things.

"I still have those moments when I say, 'Jeez, what crappy luck,'" Shannon admits. "But it's easier for me to handle challenges now, because they're nothing compared to what I've been through. I'm trying to move on, but I'm not trying to forget what happened to me. It's written all over my face."

FACE TO FACE WITH A GRIZZLY

BY KATHY COOK

Veering off the highway, Ann Quarterman, 28, steered her four-wheel-drive vehicle onto a steep dirt road in the mountainous area of Revelstoke, British Columbia. Seven miles in, she reached the hiking trail that would lead her and her friend Christine Bialkowski to a remote ski lodge nestled among the peaks.

Ann, an outdoor enthusiast and expert skier, was thinking of working at the lodge as a cook for the winter season. Wanting to see if the wild, untamed locale was right for her, she'd decided to hike to the interview rather than take the usual helicopter ride in. Christine, 25, had come along for the adventure.

On that rainy morning of October 1, 1994, Ann parked her vehicle by the trail entrance, and the women grabbed their packs. Ann, who was tall with brown hair and a bright smile, looked at her map. The ten-mile, six-hour hike would take them up the mountain and across a glacier to the lodge.

She strapped a can of bear repellent to a holster on her hip.

It had been given to her by a company she had done fieldwork for a few years back. She had never used it, but she knew they'd be crossing creeks where bears were known to feed. "Just in case," she said, smiling mischievously at Christine.

Christine, a petite woman with long blond hair, laughed. The two had met the year before, working at another mountain tourist hotel. Sharing a love of adventure, they became ski partners, biking companions, and fast friends.

Their hike began as a slow, uphill stroll through coniferous mountain forest. Despite their wet-weather gear, they were both soon drenched from the rain. Eventually the trail narrowed into a thin, overgrown path through steep and rocky terrain. They crawled over large rocks and jumped across shallow creeks, talking loudly to warn any bears of their presence.

Along the way they spotted bear droppings. The patches were not the usual seedy variety. *No berries*, Christine realized. *The bears are eating grass.* "They must be having a hard time finding food," she said.

Three hours into their journey, at an altitude just above 6000 feet, they climbed over a ridge and came to an alpine meadow above the tree line.

"Wow, isn't this something?" said Ann, gazing out at the valley below. Through a low-lying fog the land glowed with the changing colors of early autumn.

Still appreciating the vast view, Ann and Christine followed the curving path for a few moments. Then Ann stared into the meadow. "Christine, look! Bears!" A grizzly and her two cubs were about 300 yards away.

Ann wasn't frightened. She had lived in bear country, and she knew that unless surprised, bears run away from humans.

But not this time. It took a few seconds before they realized that the bears were running toward them. Christine glanced nervously at Ann. Without trees to climb, they had limited options.

They're still so far away that they're probably running after something else, Ann thought, remembering that bears often fake attacks to intimidate intruders. But the mother bear kept coming. Leaving the cubs behind, it was charging at them with incredible speed.

The two hikers began yelling and waving their arms to intimidate the bear. When the animal didn't flinch, the women started running. Then Ann stopped.

"Don't run!" Ann yelled. She suddenly remembered that if you run, bears think you are easier prey and are more inclined to attack.

Christine slowed, and both women walked down a bank out of sight of the grizzly. Ann unlatched the bear mace from its holster and pulled the safety clip. She still didn't think the bear would actually attack. The bank blocked her view as they waited. *Please be gone,* she prayed. Then the head of the grizzly popped up over the ridge just fifteen feet away.

Ann aimed her mace and waited. *I have one chance to do this right,* she thought as the bear closed in. Five feet away, the seven-foot animal rose up on its hind legs, towering over her. Their eyes locked. Ann froze, mesmerized by the fierce black stare. Then she pressed the trigger, unleashing a burning red spray into the bear's face.

Reeling in pain, the grizzly dropped to the ground and ran right past her. Ann breathed a sigh of relief. *Gone!* Then she remembered Christine, who was behind her. Ann turned around.

Before Christine could even react, the grizzly ran right at her and clamped its teeth onto her left arm. Taking her elbow deep within its jaws, the bear started savagely thrashing her back and forth. At 115 pounds, Christine was powerless against its tremendous might. She knew she was about to die.

I have to do something, Ann thought desperately. She ran over and maced the bear again.

Raging, the bear threw Christine aside and lunged at Ann. She tried the spray a third time. To her horror the can was empty.

Clamping huge teeth around Ann's outstretched right arm, the grizzly knocked her over. Together they rolled down an embankment, Ann screaming in pain. She could smell the animal's stench and felt her arm being ripped open.

At that moment her mind cleared of panic, and everything she had learned about bears came flooding back. *I have to play dead,* she realized, *or the bear will never leave me alone.*

Pulling her ravaged arm free, Ann rolled onto her stomach, trying to protect her vital organs. But the grizzly bit into her side and flicked her over. Ann flipped back onto her stomach, put her hands behind her neck and lay still.

The grizzly clawed at her backpack and bit along her sides. Then in one violent swipe, a powerful paw with three-inch claws slashed through the hood of her rain gear and the baseball cap she was wearing, peeling away a large chunk of her scalp.

Christine crouched in the bushes where the bear had thrown her. I can't sit here and watch Ann be mauled to death, she thought. If we're going to die, I'll at least put up a fight.

"I'm coming, Ann!" she yelled. As she approached the bear, she thought, I have to get it away from Ann's head.

Wearing hiking boots that were only slightly sturdier than running shoes, Christine kicked the bear's head. The force of the kick made her lose her balance, and she fell onto her back.

Christine kicked frantically, her legs flailing in the air. Then, recalling that the snout is the bear's most sensitive spot, she gave the grizzly a swift, solid kick in the nose.

The bear recoiled, then sank its teeth deeply into Christine's hip. With a final huff, the grizzly released its grip and ran downhill behind some bushes and out of sight.

Christine raised herself up and saw Ann lying still and silent, her head and torn clothing soaked in blood. "Ann, are you all right?" she asked.

"I'm playing dead," Ann whispered. "Is it gone?"

"Yes," Christine assured her.

Ann lifted her head to look, and Christine winced, seeing a chunk of Ann's scalp flap up and fall back on her blood-soaked head.

"Let's get out of here," Christine said, "before it comes back."

In Ann's pack was a small first-aid kit and some clothing. Ann's right arm and Christine's left arm were mangled and useless, but together they managed to bandage their wounds and to wrap Ann's head with a shirt. Then they discussed what to do.

They were wet, badly injured, and losing blood. It was drizzling, and the temperature was just above freezing. When the sun went down, the rain would turn to snow. They could die of hypothermia.

Christine thought of the owners of the lodge. They had said they might hike down the trail and meet Christine and Ann. If the women didn't show up, the owners might keep walking to this meadow and get attacked themselves.

"Maybe we should keep going up to the lodge," Christine said.

"It's uphill across a glacier," Ann argued. "And there's no way I'm walking back into that meadow."

"You're right," said Christine. Dumping supplies to lighten their packs and alert the owners if they came by, the two women started the hike back to Ann's vehicle.

Trying to stay coherent—and to make enough noise to warn bears—they talked and sang. Christine asked Ann about the signs of shock.

"Well, first you feel weak," replied Ann.

"Yup, I'm feeling weak," said Christine.

"Then you feel shaky."

"Yup, feeling pretty shaky."

"Then you get really thirsty."

"Uh-huh."

The humor helped. But both women had lost a lot of blood, and the difficult trek down the mountain drained what little energy they had left.

Each could use only one arm as they descended the rocks. On one steep decline Ann lost her footing and slipped down the rock side, losing her head bandage. She hauled herself up and, with Christine's help, retied the bandage. They continued on.

Halfway down, Christine noticed a trail of blood trickling from Ann's arm. To slow the bleeding, she said, "Ann, maybe we can sling your arm a little higher." But Ann could not lift it. The pain was too great.

Ann was getting weaker, and her spirits dwindled after every turn with still no vehicle in sight. "I don't think I can make it," she said, crying. "If I don't make it, tell my sister and my nieces that I love them. And my brother-in-law too."

"You can tell your family yourself when we get back," Christine reassured her.

As the miles passed, Ann's breathing became more labored. Christine urged her on. "We're almost there," she would say. "Just a couple more bends."

Slowly Ann forced one foot in front of the other. Then the vehicle was in sight. Ann bent to unlock the door, and the blood that had pooled in her raincoat splashed to the ground. Christine steered with her good right arm while Ann in the passenger seat used her good left arm to change gears. Carefully they descended the winding mountain road.

Just before the main highway, they saw a man cutting wood. "We've been attacked by a grizzly!" they called out. "Could you take us to the hospital?" His face turned ashen when he saw the blood-soaked women.

Only a few hundred feet away a road crew was repairing a bridge. Sandy Patterson was controlling traffic when the logger ran up. "You gotta help!" he shouted. "I've got two girls here who've been attacked by a bear!"

Sandy called to René Cumin, a crew member with first-aid training. While Sandy ran to radio for an ambulance, René walked over to the vehicle. "I took first aid," he said. "I failed, but I think I can help you."

Christine and Ann exchanged glances and laughed with relief. Their ordeal was over.

Ambulances whisked the injured women to the hospital in Revelstoke. There Ann Quarterman received some 50 stitches. After extensive physiotherapy she regained the use of her arm, although she did lose some muscle tissue.

The bear's attack on Christine Bialkowski narrowly missed a major artery in her hip. She, too, needed about 50 stitches on her arms and legs. The scars don't let her forget what happened, but she has fully recovered.

Ann accepted the job at the ski lodge, where she met a man from Colorado whom she plans to marry. Meanwhile, Ann and Christine remain friends.

The trail the two women took remains open to hikers. There have been no more maulings in that area.

IN THE JAWS OF A POLAR BEAR

BY ROBERT KIENER

The massive polar bear lumbered along the rocky shoreline, just a yard or so from the stormy waters of the Arctic Ocean. Occasionally it raised its head to sniff the Arctic air, hoping perhaps to pinpoint an easy meal of a washed-up ringed seal or walrus carcass.

It was late July, and in this uninhabited part of the Norwegian archipelago of Svalbard, high above the Arctic Circle and just 600 miles from the North Pole, much of the drift ice had melted. This made hunting for seals—a polar bear's favorite meal—nearly impossible. Although huge, the bear was desperately hungry.

With a westerly wind at its back, the male bear continued to patrol the shore. Then, perhaps catching the scent of something unusual, it stopped dead in its tracks. It sniffed the air, and steam billowed out of its bright black snout. Following its nose, so sensitive that some say it can smell a decaying whale carcass from 20 miles away, the bear suddenly turned downwind and inland. Its paddlelike paws dragged, leaving deep tracks in the sand. The predator was closing in on its prey.

It was to be the adventure of a lifetime. For almost two years, longtime friends Sebastian Plur Nilssen and Ludvig Fjeld, both 22, had been training for this two-month-long kayak expedition. Hoping to follow in the footsteps of other Norwegian explorers such as Roald Amundsen and Thor Heyerdahl, the two were attempting to become the first kayakers to paddle around the entire Svalbard archipelago, a trip of more than 1,100 miles through one of the world's most remote regions.

To get fit, they had donned dry suits and kayaked through the ice-filled rivers near their hometowns outside Oslo, pulled heavy kayaks over ice floes, and jumped into the freezing waters to toughen themselves.

Lifelong hunters, they honed their marksmanship by sprinting up hills, loading their rifles, and pulling the triggers. As many Arctic experts had told them, if they needed to defend themselves from a polar bear, they'd have little time to think. Each carried a rifle in a waterproof bag lashed to their kayaks. Holding steady, controlling their breathing, aiming, shooting: It all had to be second nature.

The two pioneers set out from Longyearbyen, dubbed the northernmost settlement in the world, on July 5, 2010. They averaged about 15 miles a day, and by the end of July, they had reached the northern shore of Nordaustlandet, one of Svalbard's High Arctic islands.

With the wind picking up and the sea growing choppy, they

decided to head for shore and camp on a beach near a promontory named Ekstremhuken. As Nilssen paddled alongside Fjeld, he held up the map and joked, "Funny name for a place, no? I wonder if that means something 'extreme' will happen here?" Fjeld smiled.

After pulling their kayaks onto the rocky beach, they pitched their tent and rigged up a trip-wire perimeter nine feet away, as they did at every campsite. A series of small explosive charges would go off if an animal were to cross the wire, giving the men time to grab their rifles and scare away a bear or, if necessary, shoot it.

The two awoke the next day to ferocious winds and rough seas. After checking the weather forecast via satellite phone, Nilssen and Fjeld discussed the situation. "We'll have to stay another night," Nilssen said. "Tomorrow should be clear."

Later that day, while chasing a tarp that had blown away, Nilssen fell over the trip wire, setting off an explosive charge. He quickly fitted a new one to the wire.

"Damn," he said as he crawled back inside the tent, "I'm getting clumsy in my old age." As they did every night before they tucked in, Nilssen and Fjeld double-checked that their rifles were loaded and close at hand.

As they were sound asleep, the polar bear that had picked up their scent began lumbering toward the camp.

With the wind howling, the bear burst through the trip wire, but the charge did not fire. Nilssen awoke to a crashing sound when the bear trampled the tent and ripped it to shreds with a mighty sweep of its paw. "Bear!" shouted Nilssen as he felt it lock its jaws onto the back of his skull, pulling him from his sleeping bag. All he could see was a towering mass of white fur. As the bear sank its teeth deeper into his skull, it uttered a low-pitched, guttural growling.

Nilssen was able to grab his pump-action shotgun while the bear dragged him out of the tent. Screaming, he tried to hit the bear with one hand while gripping the gun with the other. But nothing deterred the animal.

Suddenly the polar bear changed its hold on Nilssen and sank its teeth into his right shoulder. Then it shook him back and forth, each time penetrating Nilssen's flesh more deeply with its teeth. Pain shot through his body as if an ice pick were being twisted into his shoulder.

It's trying to shake me unconscious, thought Nilssen. The bear began dragging him onto the rocky beach. The shotgun is my only chance, he thought. Just then the gun fell from his grip, and the bear stepped on it, snapping it in two. "I'm dead," Nilssen said out loud when he heard the gun break in half. "It's over."

Fjeld woke up when he heard Nilssen scream and turned to see the bear inside the tent, with Nilssen's head in its jaws. While shaking him, the bear had stomped on their gear, much of which was now crushed or buried in the soft sand.

Fjeld jumped up and reached for his grandfather's World War II rifle. It was missing. He frantically clawed at the debris in front of the tent. "Where is it?" he yelled, then felt the stock of the rifle and pulled it out of the sand. "Sebastian!" he yelled. Sebastian didn't answer.

The bear was now by turns dragging and carrying Nilssen

by his wounded shoulder. I must act now to save my friend, thought Fjeld. Time was running out.

The bear dropped Nilssen some 100 feet beyond the camp. Then it roared and raked its razor-sharp claws over Nilssen's torso. Blood covered the kayaker. The bear put its two front paws on Nilssen's chest, pinning him to the ground and pushing him deep into the sand. Nilssen felt his ribs cracking. The bear's hot breath was on his face. He looked directly into its deep black eyes. They were cold and empty.

Then the bear turned and saw Fjeld standing with rifle raised outside the tent. Fjeld held his breath to still his shaking trigger finger and aimed at the bear. "Steady," he repeated to himself. He was afraid he would hit his friend. Nilssen yelled, "Shoot! Shoot!" But before Fjeld could fire, the bear climbed off Nilssen, sunk its jaws into the back of his skull again, and stood straight up, lifting Nilssen several feet off the ground.

Fjeld ran closer to them. Nilssen shouted again, "Shoot! Shoot or I die!"

The polar bear stood sideways to Fjeld; he aimed at its back and squeezed off a shot. The bullet ripped into the bear, and the animal dropped Nilssen to the sand. One last time the bear managed to sink its teeth into Nilssen's shoulder. Then Fjeld pumped four more rounds into the beast's chest. The bear fell over, dead at last.

Fearful that other polar bears might be attracted by the smell of blood, Fjeld slammed another five-shell clip into the gun. Nilssen lay crumpled on the beach. The back of his scalp hung loose and his shoulder was shredded open. His body was covered with bleeding wounds, but he was alive.

Fjeld carried him back to the tent; he covered his bleeding scalp and shoulder with compression bandages and wrapped him in a sleeping bag. "You'll make it," he told Nilssen as he gently wiped blood from Nilssen's face. "We'll get you out of here."

Nilssen groaned. His body throbbed with pain, and the smell of his blood filled the tent. He whispered to Fjeld, "My neck. I think the bear might have broken it."

Fjeld knew he had to keep Sebastian warm because it would be hard to survive the frigid temperature with such devastating wounds. He punched the number of a Longyearbyen hospital into the satellite phone. The operator picked up.

"We need help," Fjeld blurted out. "We are kayakers," he told the hospital's nurse manager, Aksel Bilicz. "My friend has been attacked by a polar bear. Please hurry!"

Bilicz called the local police, and about 35 minutes later, a rescue helicopter was in the air. The trip to the camp, however, would likely take almost an hour and a half.

Fjeld returned to Nilssen's side. Nilssen was pale and shivering. Fjeld talked to him incessantly to keep him awake. "They are sending a helicopter," Fjeld repeated. "It won't be long." Though Nilssen writhed in pain, Fjeld made the hard decision to withhold a dose of the morphine they carried with them because it might knock Nilssen out. Despite his suffering, Nilssen did not want to lose consciousness. Meanwhile, Fjeld scanned the horizon for other polar bears, his rifle loaded by his side.

When the helicopter touched down, two medics carried

Nilssen to the chopper. He was put on a saline drip and given a painkiller, though his neck throbbed too much for a brace.

At the hospital, Nilssen underwent a three-hour operation during which surgeons removed all the damaged tissue under his wounds. His neck was badly bruised but not broken. The next day, as Nilssen lay recuperating, surgeon Kari Schroeder Hansen visited him. "Another few millimeters and the bear's teeth would have punctured your lung and crushed your skull," the doctor told him. "You wouldn't still be with us."

"I know it's common for bears to crush seals' skulls," Nilssen says now. "Lucky for me, I'm thickheaded."

Today, at home north of Oslo, where he is raising a team of sled dogs, Nilssen sips coffee with Fjeld. Nilssen unbuttons his shirt. His shoulder and torso are tracked with scars from the attack. "I'm not a religious person, but I know it was a miracle I survived," he says as he buttons up. "I also know that I owe my life to Ludwig."

Fjeld demurs, saying, "I just instinctively did what we were both trained for."

The men are considering a return expedition to Svalbard—although their families, who initially learned of the attack on a radio program, are not keen on it. When asked about the experience, Nilssen is amazingly composed. "It is our big regret that the bear had to be killed," he says reflectively. "I still think the polar bear is the most majestic animal in the world. It was just trying to survive."

CREDITS AND ACKNOWLEDGMENTS

"Super Storm," by Christopher W. Davis, *Reader's Digest*, September 2006.

"Nightmare at Navajo Lake," by Derek Burnett, *Reader's Digest*, May 2005.

"Lost at Sea," by Anita Bartholomew, *Reader's Digest*, January 2006.

"Buried Alive," by Beth Mullally, *Reader's Digest*, March 1996.

"Trapped by a Killer Firestorm," by Mark Stuart Gill, *Reader's Digest*, October 1994.

"The Tot and the Twister," by Derek Burnett, *Reader's Digest*, November 2012.

"Against the Séa," by Malcolm McConnell, *Reader's Digest*, October 1997.

"Deathfall at Denali Pass," by Peter Michelmore, *Reader's Digest*, January 1996.

"Into the Wild," by Kenneth Miller, *Reader's Digest*, June 2008.

"Lost," by Lynn Rosellinni, *Reader's Digest*, September 2008.

"Journey to the South Pole," by Todd Pitock, *Reader's Digest*, December 2009.

"Terror on the Cliff," by Kenneth Miller, *Reader's Digest*, March 2013.

"Killer Wave," by Peter Michelmore, *Reader's Digest*, August 2002.

"Jet Crash in the Jungle," by Lynn Rosellini *Reader's Digest*, January 2007.

"Dam Break," by William H. Hendryx, *Reader's Digest*, July 2006.

"One Inch from Death," by Michael Bowker, *Reader's Digest*, September 1999.

"Two Boys, Five Tons of Ice, Eighty Rescuers, and a Chain Saw," by Jeff Rennicke *Reader's Digest*, April 2009.

"Swarm!," by Gerry Johnson, *Reader's Digest*, January 1997.

"Shark Attack—On Land," by Andrea Cooper, *Reader's Digest*, July 2002.

"Cornered," by Kenneth Miller, *Reader's Digest*, April 2006.

"Face to Face with a Grizzly," by Kathy Cook, *Reader's Digest*, September 1996.

"In the Jaws of a Polar Bear," by Robert Kiener, *Reader's Digest*, March 2011.

ALSO AVAILABLE FROM READER'S DIGEST

What They Did for Love

The editors of *Reader's Digest* have collected the most powerful love stories from our archives: true tales of couples, families, friends, and even strangers reaching out and reaching deep inside in the name of romance, family, and friendship.

ISBN 978-1-62145-136-5 • $15.99 hardcover

Treasury of Joy and Inspiration

This curated collection from ninety years of *Reader's Digest* highlights how daily miracles often begin with a small coincidence, guided by a divine hand, and will inspire readers to open their eyes to the joy, faith, and miracles that are all around.

ISBN 978-1-62145-142-6 • $17.99 hardcover

Stories in Uniform

Reader's Digest has been chronicling military dramas for over ninety years. In this moving collection of our very best pieces—from World War I through the War on Terror—you'll meet ordinary people faced with extraordinary circumstances in the name of America and freedom.

ISBN 978-1-62145-063-4 • $15.99 hardcover

For more information, visit us at RDTradePublishing.com
E-book editions are also available.

Reader's Digest books can be purchased through retail and online bookstores.

Reader's
digest